D0982772

KNICKERBOCKER HOLIDAY

Knickerbocker Holiday

A MUSICAL COMEDY IN TWO ACTS

BOOK AND LYRICS BY

Maxwell Anderson

AS WRITTEN TO BE SET TO MUSIC BY

Kurt Weill

ILLUSTRATED BY ROBERT H. MUTRUX

ANDERSON HOUSE
Washington, D. C.

1938

PS3501
N28 K6
1938

Copyright, *1938*, by
Maxwell Anderson

———

Printed in the United States of America
First printing December, 1938
FIRST EDITION

NOTE

CAUTION: Professionals and amateurs are hereby warned that KNICKER-BOCKER HOLIDAY, being fully protected under the Copyright Laws of the United States of America, the British Empire, including the Dominion of Canada, and all other countries of the Copyright Union, is subject to royalty. All rights, including professional, amateur, motion picture, recitation, lecturing, public reading, radio broadcasting, and the rights of translation in foreign languages are strictly reserved. Particular emphasis is laid on the question of readings, permission for which must be secured from the author's agent in writing. All inquiries should be addressed to the author's agent, Harold Freedman, 101 Park Avenue, New York City.

AMATEUR RIGHTS

The amateur acting rights of this play are controlled exclusively by the Dramatists Play Service, Inc., 9 East 38th Street, New York City, without whose permission in writing no performance of it may be made.

MUSIC

The music in this volume is reproduced by special permission of the Crawford Music Corporation, New York, N. Y.

GEORGE BANTA PUBLISHING COMPANY, MENASHA, WISCONSIN

A Preface to the Politics of
Knickerbocker Holiday

❦ ❦

KNICKERBOCKER HOLIDAY was obviously written to make an occasion for Kurt Weill's music, and since Mr. Weill responded by writing the best score in the history of our theatre, and since the public has voted an emphatic approval at the box office, the whole venture would seem to justify itself without further comment.

But there has been a good deal of critical bewilderment over the political opinions expressed in the play, and not a little resentment at my definitions of government and democracy. I should like to explain that it was not my intention to say anything new or shocking on either subject, but only to remind the audience of the attitude toward government which was current in this country at the time of the revolution of 1776 and throughout the early years of the Republic. At that time it was generally believed, as I believe now, that the gravest and most constant danger to a man's life, liberty and happiness is the government under which he lives.

It was believed then, as I believe now, that a civilization is a balance of selfish interests, and that a government is necessary as an arbiter among these interests, but that the government must never be trusted, must be constantly watched, and must be drastically limited in its scope, because it, too, is a selfish interest and will automatically become a monopoly in crime and devour the civilization over which it presides unless there are definite and positive checks on its activities. The constitution is a monument to our forefathers' distrust of the state, and the division of powers among the legislative, judicial and executive branches has succeeded so well for more than a century in keeping the sovereign authority in its place that our government is now widely regarded as a naturally wise and benevolent institution, capable of assuming the whole burden of social and economic justice.

❦ v ❦

120930

The thinking behind our constitution was dominated by such men as Franklin and Jefferson, men with a high regard for the rights of the individual, combined with a cold and realistic attitude toward the blessings of central authority. Knowing that government was a selfish interest, they treated it as such, and asked of it no more than a selfish interest can give. But the coddled young reformer of our day, looking out on his world, finding merit often unrewarded and chicanery triumphant, throws prudence to the winds and grasps blindly at any weapon which seems to him likely to destroy the purse-proud haves and scatter their belongings among the deserving have-nots. Now he is right in believing that the accumulation of too much wealth and power in a few hands is a danger to his civilization and his liberty. But when the weapon he finds is a law, and when the law he enacts increases the power of the government over men's destinies, he is fighting a lesser tyranny by accepting a greater and more deadly one, and he should be aware of that fact.

A government is always, as Stuyvesant says in KNICKERBOCKER HOLIDAY, "a group of men organized to sell protection to the inhabitants of a limited area at monopolistic prices." The members of a government are not only in business, but in a business which is in continual danger of lapsing into pure gangsterism, pure terrorism and plundering, buttered over at the top by a hypocritical pretense at patriotic unselfishness. The continent of Europe has been captured by such governments within the last few years, and our own government is rapidly assuming economic and social responsibilities which take us in the same direction. Whatever the motives behind a government-dominated economy, it can have but one result, a loss of individual liberty in thought, speech and action. A guaranteed life is not free. Social security is a step toward the abrogation of the individual and his absorption into that robot which he has invented to serve him—the paternal state.

When I have said this to some of the youthful proponents of guaranteed existence I have been met with the argument that men must live, and that when the economic machinery breaks down men must be cared for lest they starve or revolt. This is quite true and nobody opposes emergency relief. It is the attempt to make the emergency and the relief permanent that constitutes an attack on our free institutions. The greatest enemies of democracy, the most violent reactionaries, are those who have lost faith in the capacity of a free people to manage their own affairs and wish to set up the government as a political and social guardian, running their business and making their decisions for them.

For life is infinitely less important than freedom. A free man has a value to himself and perhaps to his time; a ward of the state is useless to himself—useful only as so many foot-pounds of energy serving those who manage to set themselves above him. A people which has lost its freedom might better be dead, for it has no importance in the scheme of things except as an evil power behind the word of a dictator. In our hearts we all despise the man who wishes the state to take care of him, who would not rather live meagerly as he pleases than suffer a fat and regimented existence. Those who are not willing to sacrifice their lives for their liberty have never been worth saving. Throughout remembered time every self-respecting man has been willing to defend his liberty with his life. If our country goes totalitarian out of a soft-headed humanitarian impulse to make life easy for the many, we shall get what we vote for and what we deserve, for the choice is still before us, but we shall have betrayed the race of men, and among them the very have-nots whom we subsidize. Our western continent still has the opportunity to resist the government-led rush of barbarism which is taking Europe back toward Attila, but we can only do it by running our government, and by refusing to let it run us. If the millions of workingmen in this country who are patiently paying their social security dues could glimpse the bureaucratic absolutism which that act presages for themselves and their children they would repudiate the whole monstrous and dishonest business overnight. When a government takes over a people's economic life it becomes absolute, and when it has become absolute it destroys the arts, the minds, the liberties and the meaning of the people it governs. It is not an accident that Germany, the first paternalistic state in Europe, should be governed now by an uncontrollable dictator; not an accident that Russia, adopting a centrally administered economy for humanitarian reasons, should arrive at a tyranny bloodier and more absolute than that of the Czars. Men who are fed by their government will soon be driven down to the status of slaves or cattle.

All this was known to the political leaders who put our constitution together after the revolution against England. The constitution is so built that while we adhere to it we cannot be governed by one man or one faction, and when we have made mistakes we reserve the right to change our minds. The division of powers and the rotation of offices was designed to protect us against dictatorship and arbitrary authority. The fact that there are three branches of government makes for a salutary delay and a blessed inefficiency, the elective rotation makes for a government not by cynical professionals, but by normally honest and fairly incompetent amateurs. That was exactly what the wary old founding fathers wanted, and if we are wise we shall keep it, for no scheme in the history of the world has succeeded so well in maintaining the delicate balance between personal liberty and the minimum of authority which is necessary for the free growth of ideas in a tolerant society.

M.A.

New City, Rockland Co., N.Y.
  Nov. 7, 1938.

KNICKERBOCKER HOLIDAY had its first performance on any stage, in the Bushnell Memorial Theatre, Hartford, Conn., on Saturday, September 26, 1938, when the drama was produced by the Playwrights' Co., Inc., with the following cast in order of appearance.

WASHINGTON IRVING	*Ray Middleton*
ANTHONY CORLEAR	*Harry Meehan*
MISTRESS SCHERMERHORN	*Edith Angold*
VANDERBILT	*Francis Pierlot*
ROOSEVELT	*George Watts*
DE PEYSTER	*Charles Arnt*
DE VRIES	*John E. Young*
VAN RENSSELAER	*James Phillips*
VAN CORTLANDT, JR.	*Richard Cowdery*
TIENHOVEN	*Mark Smith*
SCHERMERHORN	*Howard Freeman*
BROM BROECK	*Richard Kollmar*
TENPIN	*Clarence Nordstrom*
TINA TIENHOVEN	*Jeanne Madden*
PIETER STUYVESANT	*Walter Huston*
GENERAL POFFENBURGH	*Donald Black*

CITIZENS OF NEW AMSTERDAM: *Helen Carroll, Jane Brotherton, Carol Deis, Robert Arnold, Bruce Hamilton, Ruth Mamel, William Marel, Margaret MacLaren, Robert Rounseville, Rufus Smith, Margaret Stewart, Erika Zaranova, William Wahlert.*

SOLDIERS: *Albert Allen, Matthias Ammann, Dow Fonda, Warde Peters.*

INDIANS: *The Algonquins.*

KNICKERBOCKER HOLIDAY

ACT ONE

Act One

SCENE & & W<small>ASHINGTON</small> I<small>RVING</small> *is seated at his desk in a little study to the right of the footlights, writing with a quill. It is night, and a shaded candle lights his work. The window toward the stage is dark. As the curtain rises* I<small>RVING</small> *lays down his pen, takes up his manuscript, tears it in pieces and hurls it to the floor.*

Irving. Gossip, whisperings, intimate details of scandal,
　　And, when that well runs dry,
　　Invented rumors tricked out to start tongues wagging
　　In the coffee houses of John Street!
　　Pah! Bah! I'm no longer a child!
　　I'm Washington Irving, and the cycle of years
　　Has come round to 1809—
　　Which means that I'm twenty-six years old
　　And have as yet written nothing, that is, nothing
　　Worthy to endure!
　　I'll no more of it!
　　I've filled my last gossip column,
　　And the space may gape empty tomorrow morning!
　　A man can't go on forever
　　Manufacturing fiddle-faddle
　　For the transient amusement of the witless.
　　Yet when I throw out a hint
　　That I shall try my hand at something more ambitious
　　My friends gather round with a great wagging of craniums:
　　"Now, Irving, don't go high-and-mighty!
　　This is a pioneer country,
　　With no literature, no traditions, nothing mellow enough
　　To make an inspiring tipple for the generations!
　　Content yourself," they say; "here you are,
　　A wise and witty young dandy,
　　A man about town with a rising reputation
　　For a saucy tongue and all the latest answers!
　　Content yourself. You amuse folks over the breakfast table.
　　　Keep it up!"

Well, my friends, why not make a tradition?
A literature has to begin sometime,
And a pioneer country can't remain pioneer forever.
"Don't be heavy," they say. "Don't lose your following."
But why shouldn't a book be both good and amusing?
That's what the best of them arrived at, and I'll aim at it, too.
There's that history of Old Dutch New York I thought of
    writing;
My Knickerbocker History.
If it's funny enough it will be read;
If it's good enough it will endure—
And in all the history of the world
There's never been such a gathering
Of Pantalunatics
As among those first fat Dutch settlers.
Of course, for the sake of popularity
I'd be careful to keep the laughter innocent.
There was a seamy side even to that isle of the blest, the old
    New Amsterdam;
I'd have to gloss that over a bit here and there—
Just here and there—
Or I'd offend a lot of tony descendants
Among our High Dutch aristocracy,
And that, beyond question, would affect sales—and adversely.
But I'll avoid that—
I'll make it all enchanting romance and good clean fun!

[*He rises and sings.*]

I'll sing of a golden age
    In the history of New York
When the site of Trinity Parsonage
    Was a pasturage for pork.
When Wall Street was indeed a wall
    And the Bouerie was a farm,
And the pipe you smoked, if you smoked at all,
    Was twice as long as your arm.

(There's an idea—they should have pipes—church-wardens like this. Six hundred people in New York at that time, and now we're almost as big as Boston.)

I'll sing of an age forgot
    Before the inflation came,
When the island called Manhattan brought
    A sum embarrassing to name.
Of the days before the Indian tribes
    Had turned to wood or reservations,
Before a wigwam suggested bribes
    Or had other unsavory political connotations.

(No, I'll cut that out. No politics. I won't mention municipal graft or anything derogatory. This book has to sell!)

[The lights now begin to show the Battery at dawn as seen from the water-front. In the foreground and to the left a number of piles roped together suggest a pier, and in the rear a row of five or six peaked houses represent the city. A cannon thrusts out from a wall of the fort to the left rear. A gallows stands in the center. At the right there are a few benches, an outdoor table, and a number of bowling balls.]

Irving. I begin to see it.
Yes, I think I begin to see it—
The Battery,
Circa 1647—
Stone piers along the waterfront,
Windmills in the distance,

Perhaps a ship at anchor
Behind the rows of houses
With their corrugated roofs—
And then dawn flushing up over ancient Brooklyn—
Little Dutch Maidens washing the steps,
A trumpeter coming through—

[CORLEAR *enters left, blowing his bugle. He crosses and stands below* *gallows.*]

Corlear. Oyez! Oyez! Can the city of New Amsterdam hear me? No news by land—no news by sea—absolutely no news what-soever!

[*He goes up steps to fort and stands on parapet.* MISTRESS SCHERMER-HORN *enters down right and crosses out left driving two turkeys before her. The* CHORUS OF DUTCH MAIDENS *come out to wash the steps.*]

Chorus

[*Singing*]

Clickety-clack, clickety-clack, swish,
Slippety-slap, slippety-slap, slosh,
Swing the mop and wield the brush,
Wring the cloth and swab the dish,
     Clickety-swish, clip, clap,
     Slippety-slosh, slip, slap,
And ever
Look over
Your shoulder
Together
     For there may be coming along
     Any day, singing a song,
     Just the one handsome rover
     Who's your own destined lover;

You never can tell,
So it's just as well;
    It may make him bolder
    To glance over
    Your shoulder,
You never can tell—
So it's just as well.

Clickety-clack, clickety-clack, swish,
Slippety-slap, slippety-slap, slosh,
Set the sanding stone awash,
Soap the brush and make a wish,
    Clickety-swish, clip, clap,
    Slippety-slosh, slip, slap,
And ever
Look over
Your shoulder
Together,
    For the kingdoms under the sun
    Hold the unavoidable one,
    And in time he'll discover
    He's your own destined lover;
But give him a chance,
An occasional glance;
    If he should pass by you
    And fail to
    Descry you—
        (Oh, misery.)
    You never can tell.

[*The* GIRLS *return into the houses as* THE COUNCIL *enters.* VAN CORT-
LANDT, JR., *lights their pipes as* IRVING *sings.*]

Irving. Behold the bulging council of the city,
  These grave and solemn elders,
  Chosen, like all city councils,
  For their weight and density,

The incredible dilatoriness of their deliberations,
The impenetrable intransigence of their opinions,
But more especially for the inordinate breadth of their views
    and bottoms,
And for their intolerance of any corruption
In which they have no share.

> [*The* CouncilMEN *have seated themselves on the steps.* CORLEAR *blows his trumpet.*]

Corlear. Oyez! Oyez! News! Now ve got news! I see a ship on the bay!—Seems to be coming this way!

de Peyster. Mynheer Tienhoven! Mynheer Tienhoven! A ship comes in!

Roosevelt. Tienhoven! Tienhoven! Governor Stuyvesant comes!

> [TIENHOVEN *enters from house left and crosses to center of* THE COUNCIL.]

Van Rensselaer. Could be Governor Stuyvesant's ship, you tink?

Vanderbilt. Could be! It got to be!

de Peyster.
> [*Jumping up.*]

Den it's a holiday!

Vanderbilt.
> [*Jumping up*]

It ain't only von kind of a holiday, it's maybe tree kinds!

Van Rensselaer. Tree kinds?

de Vries. I got it down two only!

Tienhoven. Sid down! Sid down! Come to order!

Vanderbilt. Vindy Friday, Hanging Day—and Der Governor—

Tienhoven. Come to order and hush up so ve could be silent! Come to order! Answer up your names! Van Rensselaer.

Van Rensselaer. Hier.

Tienhoven. de Vries.

de Vries. Hier.

Tienhoven. de Peyster.

de Peyster. Hier.

Tienhoven. Van Cortlandt, Jr.

Van Cortlandt, Jr. Here, sir.

Tienhoven. Vanderbilt.

Vanderbilt. Hier.

Tienhoven. Roosevelt.

Roosevelt. Hier, py golly.

Tienhoven. Zhentlemen of der council, ve haf seen dot ship and der new Governor gomes in maybe a half-a-hour, and it's a national holiday mit a national celebration, and somebody got to be hanged up in style, because suppose der new Governor gomes and nobody is hanged on Hanging Day, vich falls on Vindy Friday, dot's a shame to us for a civilized nation, not to keep discipline under der cidy charder!

Van Rensselaer. Ja, ve got to hang a man!

de Peyster. Dot's true!

Roosevelt.
> [*Rising.*]
Vy haf ve got to hang a man?

Tienhoven. Hush up! Vich man ve gonto hang and how ve gonto hang him so it hurts more?

Roosevelt. Vy haf ve got to hang a man?

Van Cortlandt, Jr. Should we hang a Quaker or maybe a Baptist?

de Peyster. Last time ve hang a Baptist he folds up and dies too quick. Quakers is tougher.

Tienhoven. For der new Governor ve should give him der best, so maybe ve should hang a Quaker.

de Vries. How many Quakers ve got left?

de Peyster. Two. Very tough men. Preachers.

Tienhoven. Vouldn't die too hasty?

de Peyster. No, no. Dey kick maybe half-a-hour.

de Vries. For long time dying Quakers is on average every time der best.

Roosevelt. I said vy do ve got to hang a man? Do I get a answer?

Tienhoven. Hush up! Ve gonto drop him by der neck or pull him up from der ground?

Roosevelt. Vy is it got to be a hanging for der celebration? Could I find oud or couldn't I find oud?

Tienhoven. Give.

> [VAN CORTLANDT, JR. *gives* ROOSEVELT *money.*]

Roosevelt. I got money but I don't got no answer.

de Peyster.
> [*Coming forward*]
You know vot's a hanging?

Roosevelt. Ja, I know dot.

de Peyster. You know vot's a investigation?

Roosevelt. Ja, I know dot.

de Peyster. Vell, hangings keeps away investigations.

Roosevelt. Vot is it ve did so ve vouldn't vant to be investigated?

The Council. Hush.

Roosevelt. I said vot is it ve did, and I make a pause for answer? Honest men vouldn't be scared for investigations! I vould not be quiet! I vould not be silent! I vould vant to know who done someting!

Tienhoven. Give.

[VAN CORTLANDT, JR. *gives more money to* ROOSEVELT.]

Roosevelt

[*Sings*]

Ven you first come to session
    For making of der laws
        You liff on der salary only
But you don't make no impression
    And you don't get no applause
        And der guilders dey look so lonely,
So you maybe ask a question of a fellow standing by
And he nefer gives a answer, and he nefer makes reply
But he slips a little silver and he looks you in the eye
And he says, "Hush, hush," to you.

The Council

Hush, hush, hush hush, hush hush ush ush ush ush
Hush hush, hush hush to you!
Ve vouldn't said it's lying and ve vouldn't said it's true
But ve said hush hush, hush ush ush ush ush ush
Ve said hush hush to you!

Roosevelt

Ven you first make inquiry
    Concerning of der laws
        You really truly vant some information,
You look pretty fiery
    And you make a little pause
        And you vait for a explanation.

& 11 &

Now it's no good expecting anybody makes reply
But it's anyway a income every time you're asking why
So you're asking, so they're giving, so you're living
               pretty high,
So they're saying, "Hush hush," to you.

The Council

Hugh hush, hush hush, hush hush ush ush ush ush
Hush hush, hush hush to you!
Ve vouldn't said it's lying and ve vouldn't said it's true
But ve said hush hush, hush ush ush ush ush ush
Ve said hush hush to you!

Tienhoven. Den ve hang a Quaker, and it's a verdict. Make der announcement!

[SCHERMERHORN, *the town marshal, enters from the right, in full regalia, with massive keys at his belt. A few stragglers follow him in.*]

Schermerhorn. Vait! Vait! I would vish to speak private mit der president of der council!

Tienhoven. Speak it oud loud. Dis is a holiday.

Schermerhorn. Vell den, der is nobody to hang.

Tienhoven. Vy nod?

Schermerhorn. Der is nobody in der jail.

Tienhoven. Vy nod? Der vas plendy yesterday!

Schermerhorn. Dey vent out trough der hole.

Tienhoven. Vot hole?

Schermerhorn. Der hole in der jail!

Roosevelt. Is der a hole in der jail?

Schermerhorn. Is der a hole in der jail? I told you last December der vas a hole in der jail, only nobody goes out den because it vas cold vedder.

Tienhoven. Vy didn't you fix it?

Schermerhorn. Is it my business to fix holes in jails? Never! Am I a carpenter? No.

Roosevelt. How many escapes, py golly?

Schermerhorn. Led me see.

   [*He counts on his fingers.*]

Der vas der Quakers vot preached in der streets, vich is atheism; der vas two Moravians, desperate garachters, convigted of hideous business pragdices, vouldn't give credit; der vas a Svedish egsplorer, found guilty of discovering lands in der name of Sveden, vich is high treason; der vas tree pirates from Connecdicut, caught bloody-handed stealing goods mitout a license in Nyack and Kakiat. Dey all got out, trough der hole.

Vanderbilt. Couldn't you vatch dem?

Schermerhorn. Vy should I vatch dem? Dey never vanted to get oud before.—No, dey vent oud because today vas Hanging Day, and nobody told me!

Vanderbilt. Don't you know today vas Hanging Day?

Schermerhorn. How could I know, ven nobody ever tells me anyting? Vonce I had a prisoner used to cut notches every day, so ven I vant to know vot day it vas I go look at his notches. But he got oud! Everyday he cut notches bigger and bigger till the last time he cut a notch right trough and vent oud. Dot's how der hole got dere. And now I never know vot day is next, and nobody ever tells me!

de Vries. Der is nobody to hang?

Schermerhorn. Nobody.

Van Cortlandt, Jr. That's awful.

Van Rensselaer. Derrible.

Tienhoven. Ve got to find somebody to hang because der Governor gomes, and anyway ve made a law!

de Peyster. Ve got to find somebody!

Vanderbilt. Maybe the criminals didn't run far yet. Maybe ve could ketch von!

de Peyster. Maybe if ve could sneak down by der vater-front very soft, maybe ve could ketch even a pretty good von!
  [*They start to tip-toe out.*]

The Council. Ja!

Tienhoven. Only look like you vasn't looking! Vistle!

  [THE COUNCIL *exits, whistling.*]

Irving. And now I must have a hero, of course—
  Preferably from the lower classes—
  Rather bedraggled, if possible,
  And fairly ordinary, at first glance;

  [BROM BROECK *enters.*]

  But as you get to know him better
  You find that he's not ordinary at all—
  No, he has a definite peculiarity
  That gets him into insoluble difficulties
  In spite of the best of intentions.
  Yes, that's the fellow.

  [*He indicates* BROM.]

Brom. Poor sort of hero I turn out to be! No money, no job, no social graces! You might at least give me a good family background!

Irving. No, I want you the way you are.

Brom. Well, why do I have to have the worst disposition this side of Kingdom Come? Do you realize I've quarreled with every influential person in town?

Irving. You wouldn't be that way if I didn't have a reason for it, of course!

Brom. Well, I hope it's a good one, because I don't like myself at all—not a little bit—

Irving. Come, come, get on with the story!

Brom. All right!

[*Signals off left to* TENPIN. TENPIN *enters with a grindstone.* BROM *speaks to* CORLEAR *who appears on the fort.*]

Corlear!

Corlear. Vot is it?

Brom. Tenpin and I are going into the knife-sharpening business and we want an announcement made. Can you do that for us?

Corlear. Der usual fee is von guilder.

[BROM *tries his pockets.*]

Brom. Better forget about the whole matter. Oyez! Oyez! Who wants a knife sharpened? In fact who wants anything done? Any job, any price, any time!

[TWO GIRLS *enter from down right and* TWO MORE *from down left.*]

1st Girl. Oh, it's Brom! And Tenpin!

2nd Girl. Brom—where have you been?

3rd Girl. You shouldn't be here, you know. Mynheer Tienhoven says you're a very destructive young man and should be punished severely.

Brom. I know, but I've reformed. I'm never going to make trouble again. I'm going to keep out of fights and be very subservient and get along the way other people do.

1st Girl. Now Brom—

Brom. Yes, I am. I want to get married and before you get married you have to be civilized.

2nd Girl. You must have done very well if you're thinking of getting married.

Brom. No, but things will have to get better soon—look at me!
[*He sings.*]
   The bird flies east,
   The bird flies west,
   But he pays no rental where he builds his nest,
   And I run my business
   Identically
   No assets, no capital, nothing but me.

   When your shoes need soling, and you're standing on the
                              town,
   And your girl says please forget her,
   When you're on rock bottom, and you can't go down,
   Any change is for the better.
   When your job folds up, and your pants wear thin,
   And you're down on the bottom looking up at the top,
   When you're at zero, when you're a has-been,
   Then there's nowhere to go but up!
   To the man who has a plenty any change is for the worse,
   So he plays a losing hand against the universe,
   But in wintry weather, when the leaves turn brown,
   And you think of putting poison in your cup,
   When you're on rock bottom, and you can't go down,
        Can't go her way,
        Can't go his way,
        Can't go that way,
        Can't go this way,
   Then there's nowhere to go but up!

[TENPIN *sings.*]

   Up one street,
   And down one street,
   Wearing out the cobble-stones with my feet,

I look at tomorrow
Philosophically,
For pretty nearly everything's happened to me!

[*A group of young men enters during* TENPIN'S *song.*]

Brom, Tenpin, Boys and Girls

When your shoes need soling, and you're standing on the
town,
And your girl says please forget her,
When you're on rock bottom, and you can't go down,
Any change is for the better.
When your job folds up, and your pants wear thin,
And you're down on the bottom looking up at the top,
When you're at zero, when you're a has-been,
Then there's nowhere to go but up!
To the man who has a plenty any change is for the worse,
So he plays a losing hand against the universe,
But in wintry weather, when the leaves turn brown,
And you think of putting poison in your cup,
When you're on rock bottom, and you can't go down,
  Can't go her way,
  Can't go his way,
  Can't go that way,
  Can't go this way,
Then there's nowhere to go but up!

Tenpin.

 [*Displaying the grindstone*]

Want to see my new invention?

1st Girl.

 [*To* BROM]

Where did you go when you left the armory?

Brom. We went up north of Wall Street and began to clear a couple
of farms—but the Indians drove us out.

2nd Girl. Then what did you do?

Tenpin. We ran. I ran and Brom ran but nobody ran as fast as I did.

1st Girl. Not exactly heroic, were you?

Brom. When a man sees seventeen drunken Indians coming at him with guns he's a fool not to run.

Tenpin. I've been killed by Indians twice and I don't want to go through that again.

3rd Girl. Don't tell me that story again!

4th Girl. Will you come by every day now?

Brom. Every day. From now on I'm the town knife-sharpener.

1st Girl. I know somebody who's missed you since you went away.

Brom. I missed her, too. If you see her you might tell her.

2nd Girl. Shall I call her?

Brom. Would you?

2nd Girl.
> [*Runs over to left stage and calls up to the bay window*]
Tina! Tina Tienhoven! Somebody's come back!

1st Girl. Somebody's here again!

4th Girl. Tina! Brom's here!

3rd Girl. You'd better come down!

Tina.
> [*Looking out of bay window*]
I'm not allowed to see him! Father says he's always fighting!

Brom. But I'm a knife-sharpener now!

4th Girl. Surely you could bring out a knife to be sharpened!

Tina. Oh, maybe if you're a knife-sharpener!

[TINA *leaves the window.* VAN CORTLANDT, JR. *crosses from the billboard to* TENPIN.]

Van Cortlandt, Jr. No more sharpening knives!

Tenpin. Sir!

Van Cortlandt, Jr. There's a law against sharpening knives without a license!

[*He turns to* BROM.]

Quit sharpening knives!

Tenpin. Don't give him an order! Don't give him an order!

[*He restrains* VAN CORTLANDT, JR. *with a hand.*]

Van Cortlandt, Jr. Why not? Quit sharpening knives!

[BROM *turns.*]

Brom. Take care! Put it gently! Put it gently!

Van Cortlandt, Jr. I say quit sharpening knives!

Brom. Oh, you do, do you?

[*He drops the knife, leaps on* VAN CORTLANDT, JR., *bears him to the ground, and is busily throttling him when* TINA *runs from the house.*]

Tenpin. Brom! Brom! Don't kill him! Let him explain!

Tina. Brom! Brom!

Brom.

[*Getting up*]

Tina!

Tina. You were fighting again!

Brom. That's right! I'm sorry.

[VAN CORTLANDT, JR. *gets up.*]

I'm terribly sorry, sir. I have a weakness—I—

Van Cortlandt, Jr. Keep him away from me! Keep him away!

[*He runs out.*]

Brom. Tina!

Tina. I thought you wanted to see me, but no doubt you prefer a good street fight, any time.

Brom. Don't make it worse for me, Tina. I turned knife-sharpener just so we could exchange a word. And this has to happen, right before your eyes.

Tina. Of course, if you want to make everything impossible for us this is exactly how to do it. My father will never take you back in the armory while you go around knocking people down. Why do you fly into these terrible rages?

Brom. I knew I'd have to tell you sometime. It's a strange sort of endemic malady.

Tina. You're not ill?

Brom. No, I feel healthy.

Tina. But Brom, what possible malady could make you assault people?

Brom. I can't take orders. No matter how hard I try, I simply can not take orders from anybody.

Tina. But why?

Brom. I know you'll say this is ridiculous, but—I think maybe it was something I ate.

Tina. Don't be silly.

Brom. I'm not being silly. I was never bothered this way in Holland. I used to take orders perfectly well. No, it started in this country that winter I was out in the woods, living on wild turkey and Indian corn.

Tina. You think it might have been the wild turkey—or the Indian corn?

Brom. Yes. It gets into you somehow. It gets under your skin.

Tina. Naturally.

Brom. What I mean is as long as you stay here in New Amsterdam and eat imported stuff you're all right, but as soon as you start eating this native food, you're a menace to your superiors.

Tina. A very peculiar story. Of course, I can see that if you can't take orders, then you can't work for my father, and then you won't see so much of me—and—there's probably someone else—and—

Brom. No, no, Tina—I've been utterly miserable away from you, but—your father forgot, and gave me explicit directions, and —I hit him with something.

Tina. Was that why he was wearing a bandage?

Brom. Yes. Don't let this thing part us, Tina. Don't let it come between us forever.

Tina. I think I'd forgive you anything except not wanting me. But you've been away for weeks and no word from you.

Brom. I was trying to make myself stay away, so my curse wouldn't light on you too. But it was no use. Wherever I went I kept looking for you.

[*He sings.*]
 I've been hunting through woods,
 I've been fishing over water,
 For one certain girl
 Who's a certain father's daughter;

I've been following trails,
I've been staring after ships,
For a certain pair of eyes
And a certain pair of lips—
Yes, I looked everywhere
You can look without wings
And I found a great variety
Of interesting things—

But it never was you—
It never was anywhere you!
An occasional sunset reminded me,
Or a flower growing high on a tulip tree,
Or one red star hung low in the west,
Or a heart-break call from the meadow lark's nest
Made me think for a moment: "Maybe it's true—
I've found her in the star, in the call, in the blue!"
But it never was you—
It never was anywhere you—

Couldn't you leave your father's house and marry me—even
without his consent? We could live, you see. There's money
coming in.

Tina. My father has arranged for me to marry someone else, and he
won't tell me who it is—but let's not think about that. Let's just
hope that something will happen—and don't stay away so long
again—because—

[*She sings.*]

I've been running through rains
And the winds that follow after
For one certain face
And an unforgotten laughter;
I've been following signs,
I've been searching through the lands
For a certain pair of arms
And a certain pair of hands.

Oh, I tried a kiss here
And I tried a kiss there,
For when you're out in company
The boys and girls will pair—

But it never was you—
It never was anywhere you!

Brom and Tina

An occasional sunset reminded me,
Or a flower growing high on a tulip tree,
Or one red star hung low in the west,
Or a heart-break call from the meadow lark's nest
Made me think for a moment: "Maybe it's true—
I've found her in the star, in the call, in the blue!"
But it never was you—
It never was anywhere you—
Anywhere, anywhere you!

[TENPIN *and the* CHORUS *enter and watch* BROM *and* TINA. BROM *tries
to kiss* TINA. *She sees* TENPIN *and pulls away.*]

Tina. Everybody's looking—the girls and Tenpin—

Brom. Who cares about girls?

[*They kiss.*]
[THE COUNCIL *enters.*]

Tienhoven. Tina, to who vas you talking?

Tina. I'm talking to Brom, father,—he's back and he mends
muskets and he sharpens knives, and he's sorry he hit you over
the head, and I want to marry him.

Tienhoven. Quit talking to him!

Tina. But why shouldn't I talk to him, and why shouldn't I marry
him?

Tienhoven. I got plenty troubles, mit der new Governor goming, and nobody to hang, and right in the middle you should vant to marry a knife-sharpener!

Tina. I can't see why in the world you should have to hang anybody, even if it is a holiday! I'd like it much better if somebody got married, and I think the new Governor might like that better, too.

Brom. Couldn't you reconsider your decision, Mynheer Tienhoven? Your daughter and I have been in love for a long time, and I want nothing so much as to settle down in New Amsterdam as a law-abiding citizen. Give us your blessing, and I'll promise to make an obedient and trustworthy son-in-law.

Tienhoven.

   [*Nodding to* Brom *and then gathering* The Council *around him.*]
Vot did ve say vas der punishment for sharpening mitout a license?

Van Cortlandt, Jr. We didn't say.

Tienhoven. Couldn't be hanging?

   [*They all look at* Brom.]

de Peyster. No, no, dot couldn't be hanging.

Tienhoven. Vot did ve say vas der punishment for working on dis holiday?

   [Brom *and* Tina *go upstage.*]

Van Cortlandt, Jr. We didn't say.

Tienhoven. Couldn't be hanging?

de Peyster. No, no, couldn't be.

Tienhoven. Vot vas der punishment for breaking heads and running away from apprenticeships?

de Peyster. Maybe a year in jail.

Tienhoven. Altogeder, der tree of dem, it makes a hanging?

de Peyster. No, no. Hardly could be. Almost, maybe.

Tienhoven. Vot kind of crimes is it comes up to a hanging?

de Peyster. I got it here.

    [*He reads.*]

One. Taking away people's money. Two. Killing people. Indians you can kill. But not people. Three. Stealing a sheep. Four. Stealing a cow. Five. Stealing two pigs. One pig is not hanging. Two is. Six. Copulation with Indians.

Roosevelt. Vot? Is dot hanging?

de Peyster. Copulation with Indians. Ja, dot's hanging.

Roosevelt. I didn't know dot. Speak a liddle quieder. Maybe somebody listens.

de Peyster. Dot nobody gets hanged for, don't vorry. Copulation's at night, and witnesses dere couldn't be.

Vanderbilt. Dot's good.

de Peyster. Seven. Selling brandy to Indians.

Tienhoven. Vot? Is dot hanging?

de Peyster. Ja, hanging.

Tienhoven. Pass on, and don't say it so loud.

de Peyster. Eight. Selling firearms to Indians.

Tienhoven. Vill you hush a liddle, by der name of God? Have ve got no hanging laws except for something mit Indians?

de Peyster. Von more. Making accusations against der council.

Tienhoven. Dot's hanging?

de Peyster. Ja, hanging.

Tienhoven. Only nobody made any accusations. So dot's no good.

de Peyster. No good.

> [*They look at* BROM.]

Tienhoven. I guess maybe der best is put him in jail till ve find a law could be hanging for him.

de Peyster. Dot's der best.

Van Rensselaer. Vot should ve do? Arrest him?

de Vries. Arrest him now. Maybe ve find a law before der Governor gets here.

de Peyster. Marshal Schermerhorn, you vill arrest him.

Tienhoven. Only don't give him no orders. I know dot son-of-a-gun. He's dangerous.

de Peyster. Don't give him orders? Somebody's got to give him orders.

Tienhoven. Vell, it von't be me, I bet you.

> [*He gets behind others.*]

Schermerhorn. If somebody's got to give orders I'm the one could do it.

> [*He crosses to* BROM.]
> Brom Broeck!

Brom.

> [*Pleasantly*]
> Yes, sir.

Schermerhorn. You vas going to jail!

> [*Starts to take* BROM's *arm*]

Brom. Was I? When?

Schermerhorn. Now. Today. At vonce.

Brom.

> [*Moving close to* SCHERMERHORN]

My dear officer, whether or not you are now giving me an order is a mere matter of syntax. Do I hear you order me, positively, to go to jail?

Schermerhorn.

> [*To* THE COUNCIL]
> Do I?

Tienhoven. You bedder not.

Vanderbilt.

> [*Stepping out*]
> Is he gonto stood up and make a donkey of der law, py golly? You got to give him orders.
> [*Moves back*]

Schermerhorn. Den I do it.

> [*Crosses to* BROM]
> Vill you go to jail? Please?

Brom.

> [*Crosses to* COUNCIL—*they back a little.*]
> I hope you understand the dilemma in which we are placed, gentlemen. So long as you do not give me an order I can't see my way clear to obey you.

Schermerhorn. Ve got to maintain audhority.

Brom.

> [*Turning to* SCHERMERHORN]
> But must I sacrifice my liberty and perhaps my life to maintain your authority?

Roosevelt.

> [*Backing away still further*]
> Surdenly you haf. Vot kind of audhority you tink ve got if a fellow vouldn't go to jail even ven it's a hole in it, and additionally ve got nobody to hang because der oder fellows is too hard to ketch?

Brom. I think I have an idea. Perhaps I could solve both difficulties at once.

Tienhoven. Ven he has ideas, don't trust it.

Roosevelt. Votever it is, say it oud.

Brom. What you want most of all is a man to hang for the celebration?

Roosevelt. Dot's it.

> [*They nod assent.*]

Brom. If I find you a man who is undoubtedly guilty of a hanging offense, will you hang him?

Roosevelt. I tink so. Sure.

Tienhoven. Vait a minute.

Brom. And if you don't hang him will you let me off?

Roosevelt. I guess ve could. Who is it?

Tienhoven. Vait—vait a minute. Der is maybe a ketch in it.

Van Rensselaer. If he gives us a man ve could hang, vy not?

Brom. Are you all agreed on that?

The Council. Ja!

Tienhoven. Oh, no!

de Peyster. Unanimous, all but one.

Roosevelt. Who is dis man's name?

Brom. His name? Fellow citizens!

> [*He crosses and stands on step at center. Everyone moves toward him.*]

A few moments ago I heard it explained that selling brandy and firearms to the Indians was a hanging matter. Now when I was in Mynheer Tienhoven's employ he was constantly selling brandy and firearms to the Indians.

[*Led by* TIENHOVEN, THE COUNCIL *all move up left to escape the eyes of the crowd.*]

In fact, I left his service because I had been ordered to sell schnapps and muskets to the aborigines of Weekawken and Teaneck. It appears, therefore, that Mynheer Tienhoven is the logical candidate for the hanging and may very well celebrate the arrival of his successor by looking down upon it from a height!

The Chorus. Aha! Good for Brom!

Irving. Oh, oh!

Brom. I don't urge it. I merely allude to the facts. And now may I be excused?

Irving.
[*Stepping on to the stage*]
One moment!
[*The lights go down leaving only* BROM *and* IRVING *discernible.*]

My dear Master Broeck—
You'll really have to quit slinging mud
At the founding fathers
Or the book won't sell ten copies
And I won't make a dime.
Now, according to the sources
This Mynheer Tienhoven was guilty as hell,
But he's somebody's ancestor, and people are touchy about
   their ancestors,
So be a good fellow and gloss it over a little,
Because I'm no millionaire—
I have to make a living!
All this last part will have to come out!

Brom. That's all very well, but it happens that I live here. It's the only life I have and I must defend myself as I can.

Irving. Surely there's some escape for you

Without besmirching too many reputations!
I suggest that you leave town.

Brom. Where would I go? This New Amsterdam's a little settle-
ment of six hundred inhabitants, entirely surrounded by hostile
Indians. Outside I run into the Indians, inside I run into the
council, and God knows which is worse.

Irving. It is a predicament, I admit. But what I'm really concerned
about is your own character. I want people to like you, and in
order to like you they must understand you. And you're de-
cidedly complex. You began as a young fellow with a perfectly
fantastic dislike for orders—but how does that fit in with your
sudden attack on civic corruption?

Brom. Well, to be frank, I'm scared, and I want to get out of this.

Irving. I know that—

Brom. And about my character, it's funny you should mention that.
I was thinking about it myself. One of those last-minute résumés
when you're about to die, you know? And it occurred to me—
don't laugh at this—that maybe I was the first American.

Irving. The first American?

Brom. Yes, the beginning of a national type. The kind of person
that grows naturally on this soil. A person with a really fantastic
and inexcusable aversion to taking orders, coupled with a complete abhorrence for governmental corruption, and an utter in-
capacity for doing anything about it.

Irving. That's the picture of an American, certainly, and by
thunder it fits you, too! Brom, I believe you've hit on something.
You've put your finger on the one outstanding national trait. An
American is a fellow who resents being ordered around!

Brom. It's a sort of test—

Irving. At last I've got it.

Brom. And I'm right.

Irving and Brom

[*Sing*]

How can you tell an American?
    Has he any distinguishing flavor?
Could you spot him on an elephant in Turkestan
Or floating on a raft fifty miles at sea
As you'd know a single leaf from the sassafras tree
    By its characteristic savor?

It isn't that he's short or tall,
It isn't that he's round or flat,
It isn't that he's civilized or aboriginal
Nor the head-size of his hat,
No, it's just that he hates and eternally despises
The policeman on his beat, and the judge at his assizes,
The sheriff with his warrants and the bureaucratic crew
For the sole and simple reason that they tell him what
                to do;
And he insists on eating, he insists on drinking,
He insists on reading, he insists on thinking—
Free of governmental snooping or a governmental plan—
And that's an American!

How can you tell an American?
    Has he any distinguishing notion?
There's something in the essence of a good champagne
That makes you certain sure you're not imbibing rain,
And you won't succeed in growing an American man
    On the opposite side of an ocean.

It isn't that he's good or bad,
It isn't that he's gay or grim,
It's only that authority repels him as a lad
And never goes down with him.
Yes, it's just that he hates both the guts and the faces
Of the people who can order him and put him through
                    his paces,
The assessor with his taxes or the colonel at review
Or any fool official who can tell him what to do,
And he won't go to heaven and he won't go to hell,
And he will not buy and he will not sell
According to the precepts of a governmental plan—
And that's an American!

How can you tell an American
        When it comes right down to cases?
Is there any one virtue or particular vice
Like a Scotchman's whiskey or a Chinaman's rice
Or a gypsy's addiction to the moving van
        That marks him among the races?

It isn't that he's black or white,
It isn't that he works with tools,
It's only that it takes away his appetite
To live by a book of rules.
Yes, it's just that he hates and he damns all the features
Of any mortal man set above his fellow creatures,
And he'll hate the undertaker when at last he dies
If he hears a note of arrogance above him where he lies;
He does his own living, he does his own dying,
Does his loving, does his hating, does his multiplying
Without the supervision of a governmental plan—
And that's an American!

[*They shake hands.*]

Irving. Sir, I extend a hand to you across the centuries. Now that

I know you better I think I can trust you to take care of yourself most of the time.

[*Starts away, then turns*]

By the way, I hope these bloodthirsty old buzzards won't actually succeed in hanging you. An execution of this sort would make an unforgivable blot on my pages. To say nothing of the fact that I'd hate to lose you.

Brom. Thanks.

Irving. Don't mention it.

Brom. We'll have to begin where we left off, of course.

Irving. Surely, surely—only, you know, play down the corruption.

[*He returns to his desk and begins to write.*]

Tienhoven.
[*Coming down steps at left, followed by rest of* COUNCIL]
It's not true! None of it's true about Indians!
[*Everyone moves down to positions as before* IRVING'S *interruption.*]

Brom.
[*Crosses right*]
Everybody knows it's true, of course.
[*Looks at* IRVING]
However, I won't press that point.

Vanderbilt.
[*To* TIENHOVEN]
He don't believe you.

Van Rensselaer. Vot you tink—der's a ship coming in—you better go back to Holland?

Vanderbilt. I guess maybe you better, py golly.

Tienhoven. I couldn't go back to Holland. Der's a couple warrants out for me in der Hague.

de Peyster.
> [*Comes down to center of* COUNCIL *with a law in his hand*]

You wouldn't need to! You forgot something! Making accusations against der council is a hanging business! Seems to me somebody made accusations against der council here!

de Vries. Dot's true!

Vanderbilt. Den, py golly, now ve got him! And ve got him for hanging by der same bargain! Tienhoven, it's all right, ve got him!

de Vries. Dot's a good law! If somebody thought of dot, he's good!

The Council.
> [*Turning toward* BROM]

Ha, ha, ve got him!

Van Cortlandt, Jr. Do we bring in a verdict?

de Vries. Sure, ve bring in a verdict! It's a motion!

Van Rensselaer. Everybody say aye, quick!

The Council. Aye!

de Peyster. It's carried! It's a verdict!

Roosevelt.
> [*To* TIENHOVEN]

Is it fine with you?
> [VAN CORTLANDT, JR. *crosses to* BROM'S *right.*]

Tienhoven. Oh, with me it's fine.

The Council. Hang him up! Hang him up!
> [*They start toward* BROM.]

Tina. Father, father, would you hang the man I love?

Tienhoven. He vas going to hang me, vasn't he?

Tina. But you were guilty!

The Chorus. Yes, you were guilty!

Tienhoven. Not legally, I vasn't!

Tina. And he's innocent!

The Chorus. Yes, he's innocent!

Tienhoven. Not legally, he's nod!

Tina. But it's not justice!

The Chorus. No, it's not justice!

Tienhoven. Nobody said it vas justice! Ve said it vas legal!

Tina. But what are laws for, if not for justice?

Tienhoven. I tell you dot some oder time, not now.

Schermerhorn.
   [*Crosses to* BROM'S *left*]
   Should ve pull him up?

The Council. Ja!

   [TINA *motions* BROM *to run, he turns toward right stage to make an escape; and finds* VAN CORTLANDT, JR. *facing him with two pistols.*]

Brom. Oh, you're here?

Van Cortlandt, Jr. Yes, I'm here!

   [*He pushes* BROM *up left, to left corner of center step. The* GIRLS *move down right to avoid trouble.* TENPIN *jumps into center facing crowd.*]

Tenpin. Are you going to let 'em do it?

The Crowd. No!

   [*Led by* TENPIN *the* MEN *start to advance on* THE COUNCIL.]

Tienhoven. Maybe some more peoples vants to get hanged, huh?

   [SCHERMERHORN, *with a pistol in his right hand, backs toward* THE COUNCIL.]

Schermerhorn. Look oud now, look oud, I got guns ready!

   [*He turns his head and fires the gun blindly.* TENPIN *falls.*]

1st Girl. Oh, Tenpin's shot!

Tenpin.

> [*Jumping to his feet*]
> He didn't hurt me! He just bent my lucky shilling! Come on!
> Nothing can kill me! Come on!
> [*They begin to advance on* THE COUNCIL *again.*]

Tienhoven. You vant to get everybody hanged up!

Brom. Wait a minute, boys—You're not indestructible like Tenpin. I don't want anybody killed in my unworthy interest. Let the machinery of justice proceed.

> [SCHERMERHORN *ties* BROM'S *hands.*]

Tina.

> [*Going to* BROM]
> Brom, Brom! Look at me! Speak to me!

Brom. I don't dare, Tina, I must bear myself like a man. However, I leave my sharpening utensils and equipment to Tenpin—and I leave my flute to Tina Tienhoven, as a token of my undying affection.

> [*Everyone turns away.*]

Tina. Oh, if it were only undying.

> [*She takes him down left and sings.*]

> Oh, love, will you keep me in mind
>   When they've taken your life away,
> When your voice goes back to the wind,
>   And the light goes out of your day?
>   My love will cling to you,
>   My heart will sing to you,
>   Till the hair on my head is thinned
>   And my lips are gray—
>   But when you're but a memory,
> Will you, can you remember me?

Brom

Oh, love, when my eyes are gone blind,
  And the moss on my stone is gray,
And the worms on my corse have dined
  In the dark of the sunken clay,
    My love will cling to you,
    My dust will sing to you
  Till your figure is bent and thinned
  In a far-off day,
  And when I'm but a memory
Still then, even then, shall I remember thee!

Chorus

  His love will cling to her
  His dust will sing to her
Till her figure is bent and thinned,
In a far-off day,

Brom and Tina

And when you're but a memory
Still then, even then, shall I remember thee!

[*As the* CHORUS *sings,* SCHERMERHORN *takes* BROM *up to the gallows and puts the rope around his neck.* TINA *moves down left.*]

Brom.

[*Fingers the rope which has slipped down over his shoulders*]

One last request—if there's time?

Schermerhorn.
[*Looks questioningly at* The Council. *They nod assent.*]
Vot is it?

Brom. It's my wish to die quickly and easily, if you'll grant me that final boon, and therefore I beg and pray that you use the old-fashioned way of hanging, with the noose around my neck. The modern method, now in vogue in England and on the continent, may be more gratifying as a spectacle and more effective as punishment, but it's very trying to the central participant, and I don't wish my agonies prolonged.

Schermerhorn. Vot is dis modern method?

Brom. Hanging by the neck has been discarded completely in all civilized states, I believe, and hanging by the belly is now the proper mode of capital punishment, partly because the prisoner takes longer dying, which adds to the merriment of the crowd, and partly because he suffers more pain, which assists in deterring crime.
[The Council *gathers in a group down left to discuss what* Brom *has said.* Schermerhorn *joins them.*]

de Vries. Vot's dot?

de Peyster. A new vay of hanging—squeezing around der stomick.

Van Rensselaer. He likes it?

de Peyster. No, he don't like it.

Brom. Sometimes I think the more modern we are the more barbarous we become, for there's no death so lingering, so excruciating, as this latest invention of the executioner.

Vanderbilt. I pet you it hurts more!
[*He feels his stomach tenderly.*]

de Vries. If it's excruciating it hurts more!

Schermerhorn. So, you don't like dot, huh?
[*They all look at* Brom.]

Brom. It's the one thing a criminal fears!

Vanderbilt. If it's a good vay I guess maybe ve should use it.

Brom. Oh, no, gentlemen, no, no! Anything but that! Anything! Oh, I never should have mentioned it!

Schermerhorn. If it hurts more, and it lasts longer, I guess it's vot ve do.

Tienhoven. Look oud for him, he's a tricker!

Schermerhorn. Oh, no! He don't trick me!
[*Goes up to* BROM *and puts the rope firmly around his waist*]
Ve put der rope right here! And see how you like dot!
[CORLEAR'S *trumpet sounds.*]

Corlear. Governor Stuyvesant is now entering the city of New Amsterdam! Uncover your heads and lift your voices in huzzas! Governor Stuyvesant!
[*All move to see the* GOVERNOR *off right.*]

Schermerhorn. Should ve hang now, or vait for der Governor?

Vanderbilt. Here's der Governor! Ve pull him right up in der Governor's eye!
[THE COUNCIL *pull lustily on the rope and* BROM *rises in the air, swinging by the middle. The trumpet sounds, the* CHORUS *shouts.*]

The Chorus. Hurrah for Stuyvesant!
[STUYVESANT *enters with* GENERAL POFFENBURGH *and his* GUARDS, *and lifts a hand for silence.*]

Stuyvesant. Gentlemen of the council! Citizens and friends! This is a most touching performance! I—But what, in God's name, do you think you are doing with that man!

Tienhoven. Ve are hanging him on Hanging Day in honor of der new Governor!

Stuyvesant. And why is the rope around his circumference and not around his neck?

Vanderbilt. Isn't dot der new vay?

Stuyvesant. New way of what?

Vanderbilt. Isn't it der new style in Europe to hang by der belly now? Because it hurts more?

Stuyvesant. My good friends, I don't know where you picked up that highly original notion, but it's erroneous. They hang by the neck in Europe, now as always. When you want to hang, you hang to kill. This would merely make an enemy of a man!

de Peyster. He said it vas der new vay!

Stuyvesant. Oh, he said it was the new way?
[*Swinging* BROM *around to face him*]
This was your idea?
[BROM *nods his head.*]

Stuyvesant. Then I have great admiration for you, and I pardon you! Let him down!
[*They do so.*]
A young man who saves his own life so neatly should be worth saving! Moreover, there are to be no executions on this day of deliverance and rejoicing!

The Crowd. Hurrah!

Stuyvesant. Any little unpleasantness of that sort will go over till tomorrow! From now on, citizens of New Amsterdam, you will have to do with a different and, let us hope, less stupid form of government.

Vanderbilt. You said ve vas stupid?

Stuyvesant. I said you were stupid and I repeat it! No doubt you mean well, but from the reports I have had of you, and from this present proceeding, I should doubt that ever, in the history of the world, there had been a more preposterous, muddle-headed, asinine, crooked, double-dealing, venal, vicious, fat-headed group of men in charge of a nation's destiny! Hello, Tienhoven.
[*He shakes hands with* TIENHOVEN.]

People of New Amsterdam, I come to save you from them, and, I judge, just in time!

[*The* CROWD *cheers* STUYVESANT *and jeers* THE COUNCIL.]

Stuyvesant. Yes, my citizens, there is to be no more official nonsense. From this date forth the council has no function except the voting of those wise and just laws which you and I find that we need! From this date forth all taxes are abolished!

[*A tremendous cheer goes up.*]

Except for those at present in effect and a very few others which you and I may find necessary for the accomplishment of desired reforms.

[*The* CROWD *looks a little worried.*]

From this date forth every man shall be guaranteed enough to live on—

[*The* CROWD *cheers.*]

—unless it be my personal opinion that he is not worthy to live. The entire freedom of the city shall be granted to every man, woman and child—

[*They cheer once more.*]

—in return for the mere formality of registering name, place of residence, amount of income and total wealth. And lastly, there shall be no coercion used by the government toward any man, woman or child—

[*Cheers*]

—except on my personal order or the order of officers delegated by myself. In other words, citizens, you may safely put yourselves in my hands. So long as you are my friends I guarantee you good fortune, and it follows that I have no enemies. At least I hope not. Life for my enemies will be most uncertain. If I have one drawback as governor, and to be honest with you I must mention it, it is only that I am absolutely insistent on having my own way. Do not, I beg of you, make me your enemy, for I am utterly implacable; I have a long arm, a sharp eye, a good nose, and I bear grudges. The one man I cannot tolerate is the man who cannot take orders.

[*He looks at* THE COUNCIL.]

Are you with me?

[TENPIN *jumps in front of* BROM *and cheers violently to cover* BROM'S *silence. The* CROWD *cheers loudly.*]

The Crowd. Every one of us! To the last man!

Stuyvesant. Thank you. I thought so, and I'm grateful. And now— but I mentioned my nose a moment ago, and perhaps I should explain. My nose is excellent, but peculiar. Most peculiar. When there is opposition in my neighborhood I can smell it instantly.

[*He sniffs at the* CROWD.]

And I smell it now!

[*He walks slowly past the whole* CROWD *sniffing. When he gets to* BROM, *he pauses and everyone is terrified.* TINA *pushes a bouquet under his nose. He takes it, smiles and walks on.*]

Or at least I thought I did. Perhaps I was wrong. For my sake and yours, I hope so. Nothing gives me more pain than the violence which I commit when I discover the least breath of opposition to my altruistic policies. Gather round me.

[*He beckons to the* CROWD, *and sits on the small bench down right.*]

There was a native tribe in Curaçao which objected to learning the catechism of the Dutch Reformed denomination. It was perhaps too much to ask of a simple folk, but in my ungovernable fury I hardly paused to consider that aspect of the situation. No, I wiped out the entire tribe singlehanded; and in my excess of penitence, bowed with grief, broken utterly by my recollection of those charming faces which I would see no more, I retired to my solitary lodgings, took only the lightest refreshment, and touched no liquor for three days.

[*He pauses, visibly moved.*]

But enough of these depressing reminiscences! Either the wind has changed or my nose was in error. We now enter upon a new era, a future of universal happiness and abundance!

[*He sings.*]

> One touch of alchemy
>> Transmutes our age to gold;
> Would you be rich and free?
>> Then do as you are told.

Chorus

> This modern alchemy
>> Transmutes our age to gold;
> The man who would be free
>> Must do as he is told.

Stuyvesant

> No man shall want for food,
>> Nor ditto any wife;
> All hail the bright, the good,
>> The regimented life!

Chorus

> No man shall want for food,
>> Nor ditto any wife;
> All hail the bright, the good,
>> The regimented life!

Stuyvesant

The honeymoon of time
    I augur and proclaim,
The apex of our climb
    For burgher and for dame.

Chorus

The honeymoon of time
    He augurs and proclaims.
The apex of our climb
    For burghers and for dames.

Stuyvesant

All hail the political honeymoon
    Sing the news to hoi polloi,
Of each individual man his boon
    In an age of strength through joy!

Chorus

All hail the political honeymoon,
    Sing the news to hoi polloi,
Of each individual man his boon
    In an age of strength through joy!

Stuyvesant. And now I want to assure you that this is a people's
government, and that I shall take no step without consulting you.
Your future is therefore secure.

[*The* Crowd *cheers.*]

Now leave me alone with the council a moment. I have a few
decisions to make. Alone, I say! Alone!

[*The* Crowd *exits leaving* Stuyvesant *alone with* The Council.]

Stuyvesant. Last year's report, Poffenburgh.

[*He seats himself to look it over.*]

Yes, yes. Yes, yes. Someone among you has been pouring out
a steady stream of arms and gin to the Indians—not only for

years, for decades! In violation of your own statutes! Endangering even your national existence! And no doubt sharing gains with all of you, because you've all winked at it!

Roosevelt. Couldn't be true.

Stuyvesant. It is true!—Now those of you who are not guilty of this crime, all those who have done no worse, say, than take money to keep quiet, may go. Those, I say, who are not guilty!

[*One by one the members of* THE COUNCIL *steal out on tiptoe, till only* TIENHOVEN *is left. Finally* TIENHOVEN *hang-dogs toward the exit.*]

Mynheer Tienhoven.

[TIENHOVEN *pauses.*]

What was your profit from this illicit trade last year?

Tienhoven. Maybe a tousand guilder.

Stuyvesant. And the year before?

Tienhoven. Maybe almost der same.

Stuyvesant. Then you think I haven't looked into it? It was more than fifty thousand last year, and nearly the same the year before—aside from what you had to pay your friends for silence.

Tienhoven. Ja, it's expensive.

Stuyvesant. No doubt.

Tienhoven. You vouldn't hang me, maybe?

Stuyvesant. I don't know why not.

Tienhoven. So.

Stuyvesant. Except that you might be useful.

Tienhoven.

[*Hopefully*]

I could be useful?

Stuyvesant. My regime will require a good deal of ready cash. From now on the sale of drink and muskets to the savages is a government monopoly.

Tienhoven. Der government is going to commit crimes?

Stuyvesant. The government can do no wrong, Mynheer Tienhoven. The vessel on which I came brought a cargo of arms and alcoholic beverages for disposal to the Indians of the neighborhood. You will see to it.

Tienhoven. I bet you you haf to square some people.

Stuyvesant. You will continue to act as pay-off man, with the necessary hush-money at your disposal.

Tienhoven. Mine Gott in Hefen!

Stuyvesant. You flatter me. I am only a man, like yourself, but with a profound theory of government. What is a government, Mynheer Tienhoven?

Tienhoven. It's vot keeps people down.

Stuyvesant. A very loose definition. No, a government is a group of men organized to sell protection to the inhabitants of a limited area—at monopolistic prices. The more dangers there are the higher those prices are set, and it follows that the sale of weapons to the Indians, which is a danger to the community, is a positive blessing to the government.

Tienhoven. Vot a brain! Vot a brain!

Stuyvesant. However, it is necessary that the populace have certain illusions about me, and also that I have certain illusions about myself. You will conduct the necessary finnagling. I want to know nothing about the petty details!

Tienhoven. And you tink maybe I fit in all right?

Stuyvesant. Under any government there is one man who handles the cash. The pay-off man.

[*Sings*]

Huh huh huh, huh huh huh, huh huh huh!
You're the one indispensable man!
In every government
Whatever its intent
There's one obscure official with a manner innocent;
His job invisible
Is purchasing good will
With wads of public money taken from the public till.
He's the one indispensable man!

Tienhoven

[*Sings*]

I'm der von indispensable man!

Stuyvesant

There's little said about him,
But you cannot do without him,
For of governmental measures there's but one omnipotent,
It's the measure of your treasure and just where and how
                it's spent
By the one indispensable man!

Tienhoven

Huh huh huh, huh huh huh, huh huh huh!
I'm der von indispensable man!
Der governmental pocket,
No matter how you stock it,
Vill never vin elections if there's no von to unlock it;

Stuyvesant

It's really very funny
How governmental money
Transforms an opposition storm to weather calm and
    sunny!
You're the one indispensable man!

Tienhoven

I'm der von indispensable man!

Stuyvesant

The guilders spent on Sunday
Return in votes on Monday,
And although you lost the argument, with cash your point
    is proven!

Tienhoven

I've no horns; my foot's not cloven; I'm plain Mynheer
    Tienhoven,

Stuyvesant

And the one indispensable man!

Tienhoven

Yes, although I'm reprehensible,

Stuyvesant

Perhaps quite indefensible,

Tienhoven

You'll find me, if you're sensible,

Stuyvesant

Completely indispensable—

Tienhoven

Der von indispensable man!

Stuyvesant

Yes, the one indispensable man!

[*At the end of the song* STUYVESANT *and* TIENHOVEN *go into* TIEN-HOVEN's *house.* BROM *and* TINA *enter.*]

Brom. I wish we could find Stuyvesant alone.

Tina. But it's better to see them together. My father won't dare to object in front of the Governor. And the Governor said he had a great admiration for you.

Brom.

[*Sitting on the steps*]

I don't quite trust him, though. He doesn't always seem to be saying what he's thinking.

Tina. But I think he's charming. I like him very much, and I'm sure he'll speak a word to my father for us. And that will settle it, and then we can get married.

Brom. He has influence with your father, certainly, and it's worth trying.

Tina. Shall we go in?

Brom.

[*Rising*]

I'd better knock first.

[*He raps on the door.* TIENHOVEN *dashes out, pushing* BROM *aside.*]

Tienhoven. I have an announcement to make! Corlear! Blow der trumpet! Blow der trumpet!

[CORLEAR *blows, and the* CROWD *comes streaming in.*]

I have been in conversation mit my old friend Pieter Stuyvesant, der new Governor, and ve have arranged that my daughter Tina shall marry him and be der Governor's vife!

Tina. Father! I want to marry Brom!

Tienhoven. It's all fixed ub.

Tina. But he's an old man!

Tienhoven. He's a great soldier and he is Governor.

Tina. But he has a wooden leg!

Tienhoven. He has a silver leg! Solid silver!

Tina. I don't care if it's gold!

Tienhoven. You vill learn to like it. Girls geds over dese liddle tings.

Tina. What a horrible idea!

[*She sings.*]

Whatever are old people thinking of
When arranging a marriage?
They think about silver, they think about gold,
And how much your kisses will bring when sold,
And how you'll ride out in your carriage!

Council

And young people think about love! Huh, huh!

Brom and Tina

Yes, young people think about love!

The Girls and Tina

God knows what the old folks are thinking of
When a troth is plighted,

But they seemingly think
Of the kitchen sink
And what you will eat and what you will drink
And how many lids on the kitchen stove,
And the coppery pans that will glint and wink
When the candles are lighted,
With never a thought for the stars above!

The Council

And young people think about love! Huh, huh!

Brom, Tina and Girls

Yes, young people think about love!

Brom

Whatever are old people thinking of
When arranging a wedding?
They think about where you will sleep, not with whom,
And business advantages with the groom,
Or even the weave of the bedding!

The Council

And young people think about love! Huh, huh!

Brom, Tina and Chorus

Yes, young people think about love!

The Boys

God knows what the old folks are thinking of
When a troth is plighted,
But they seemingly think
Of the kitchen sink
And what you will eat and what you will drink
And how many lids on the kitchen stove
And the coppery pans that will glint and wink
When the candles are lighted,
With never a thought for the stars above!

The Council

But young people think about love! Huh, huh!

Brom, Tina and Chorus

Yes, young people think about love!

Tina

Remember your daughter will have to lie
In the bed that you're making,
Will have to lie down with that horrible peg
Strapped onto his torso in place of a leg,
In spite of her sad heart's aching!

The Council

Oh, young people think about love! Huh, huh!

Brom, Tina and Chorus

Yes, young people think about love!

The Chorus

God knows what the old folks are thinking of
When a troth is plighted,
But they seemingly think of the kitchen sink
And what you will eat and what you will drink
And how many lids on the kitchen stove
And the coppery pans that will glint and wink
When the candles are lighted,
With never a thought for the stars above,

The Council

But young people think about love! Huh, huh!

Brom, Tina and Chorus

Yes, yes!—

The Council

Huh, huh!—

Brom, Tina and Chorus

Yes, young people think about love!

The Council

Huh, huh!

Tina. I simply won't marry him, that's flat, and I won't leave Brom! ~To CROWD~

[STUYVESANT *enters from the house. There is a silence.*]

Stuyvesant.

[*Grimly*]

So young people think about love? Well, we're prepared for that emergency too! This celebration will be crowned by a feast from the ship's stores. We have brought with us a considerable supply of Holland's gin and Dutch Madeira and you will find these comestibles waiting for you on the pier.

The Crowd. Ah!

[*The* CROWD *runs out toward the pier.*]

Stuyvesant. Tienhoven! Perhaps I should have a few words with the maiden Tina.

Tienhoven. Tina! Tina! (Auyone could Do this)

[TINA *re-enters and moves slowly toward* STUYVESANT.]

Stuyvesant. Come, my dear. Do I sense a certain reluctance?

Tina. No, sir.

Stuyvesant. I hope not.

[TIENHOVEN *goes out.* STUYVESANT *and* TINA *are left alone.*]

My dear, it has been arranged for political reasons that I should espouse the daughter of Mynheer Tienhoven. But what good fortune! What astounding luck! What a face, what a figure— what a divinity among maidens! There's no princess in the courts of Europe with half your beauty or your charm!

Tina. I'm afraid you flatter me.

Stuyvesant. You haven't seen the present crop of princesses. No, I understate the case. My impression is more than favorable. I'm delighted. And now we shall make arrangements for the wedding.

Tina. The wedding?

Stuyvesant. The sooner the better, my dear Tina, the sooner the better.
[*He looks at his watch.*]
It's a little late today—but tomorrow at the latest—

Tina. Tomorrow! But we're not even betrothed!

Stuyvesant. Then we'll have the betrothal in the morning and the wedding in the afternoon—

Tina. No, no, please!

Stuyvesant. Not tomorrow?

Tina. I'm very young—I'm—not ready at all—

Stuyvesant. I should, of course, defer to your desires in such a matter. But let us understand each other. It is your father's wish that you marry me?

Tina. Yes, sir.

Stuyvesant. And you will hardly oppose your father's decision?

Tina. No, sir.

Stuyvesant. Then since it's to come sooner or later, my child, and you arouse my ardent affection, I see no point in postponement—

Tina. But don't you think you could wait—a few—years?

Stuyvesant. Years!

Tina. Yes, sir.

Stuyvesant. Years? You are young, my sweet, you have the world and a lifetime before you, but the hair is graying at my temples

—slightly—but graying—and the days begin to slip rapidly through my fingers. For my sake try to overcome your girlish modesty and let me lead you to the altar while the fire burns brightly.

Tina. A few months, then—a few weeks—

Stuyvesant. Ah, these months and weeks—

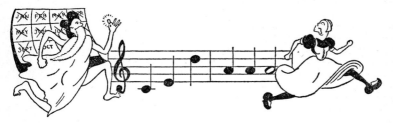

[*Sings*]
>When I was a young man courting the girls
>I played me a waiting game;
>If a maid refused me with tossing curls
>I let the old earth take a couple of whirls
>While I plied her with tears in place of pearls—
>And as time came around she came my way,
>As time came around she came.

>But it's a long, long while from May to December
>And the days grow short when you reach September,
>And I've lost one tooth and I walk a little lame,
>And I haven't got time for the waiting game,
>For the days turn to gold as they grow few,
>September, November,
>And these few golden days I'd spend with you,
>These golden days I'd spend with you.

>When you meet with the young men early in spring
>They court you in song and rhyme,
>They woo you with words and a clover ring

But if you examine the goods they bring
They have little to offer but the songs they sing
And a plentiful waste of time of day,
A plentiful waste of time.

And it's a long, long while from May to December—
Will a clover ring last till you reach September?
I'm not quite equipped for the waiting game,
But I have a little money and I have a little fame,
And the days dwindle down to a precious few,
September, November,
And these few precious days I'd spend with you,
These precious days I'd spend with you.

Stuyvesant. So you see how it is, my dear?

Tina. Yes, sir, I do see, but there was someone else—

Stuyvesant. Was there?

Tina. Yes, but I'll tell him if I have to—if I have to I'll tell him.

[*The* CROWD *re-enters and a dance begins which becomes general,* STUYVESANT *dancing with* TINA, BROM *sitting downstage near the pier, very lonely. At the height of excitement the* Boys *lift* STUYVESANT *to their shoulders. Suddenly* STUYVESANT *lifts a hand for silence. The music slips into a snarling cadence and stops.*]

Stuyvesant. Stop! Let me down! I was not mistaken!

[*He sniffs angrily.*]

Somewhere among you I smell defiance! Someone among you harbors rebellion and dissatisfaction!

[*He stumps among them, sniffing. Crosses to* BROM.]

If I had not this moment saved your life I should say it emanated from you!

Brom. I'm sorry.

Stuyvesant. You find my regime unwelcome?

Brom. No, sir, it seems quite well-intentioned and generous. Beyond all expectation. And of course I'm very grateful to you for saving my life.

Stuyvesant. Young man, I like you, and on this particular day I shall make every effort to be tolerant and forgiving. Let us discuss the matter quite openly.
  [*Moves to center of stage,* BROM *following*]
What is your objection to me?

Brom. I have a private difficulty. Something like a disease.

Stuyvesant.
  [*Stepping back*]
You have a disease?

Brom. Not exactly—

Stuyvesant. I think I know what you mean. You don't take easily to discipline.

Brom. Yes.

Stuyvesant. But I have a cure for that. A complete and thorough cure. You will receive and you will execute orders until you are worn quite smooth.

Brom. I'm afraid it won't work.

Tina. Oh, Brom, you owe your life to him! Please don't make trouble!

Stuyvesant. Be quiet! Kindly note, young man, that I am still in a gentle and lenient mood. All I ask of any citizen is that he subscribe fully and freely to my policies as announced. Can you do that?

Brom. I—

Stuyvesant. I say, can you do that? Because I still smell you very strongly!

Brom. Forgive me, sir; I have no wish to criticize, but didn't you say that every man would be guaranteed enough to live on?

Stuyvesant. I did.

Brom. It was something you said right after that which affected me.—Something about—unless it was your personal conviction that he was unworthy to live—

Stuyvesant. Would you want a man to live if he were unworthy to live?—

Brom. No, sir. It was just the notion of your deciding personally whether a man were to live that sounded arbitrary—

Stuyvesant. By the eleven thousand virgins, I begin to find your conversation disagreeable!

Brom. And then there was something about everybody registering his name and residence, and no coercion being used except on your personal order—

Tienhoven.
   [*At right of stage—to* BROM]
   Dot's true now. Vot did dot mean?

Brom. You see, all your reforms seem just and right and reasonable, and I'd want to help you with them, but—

Stuyvesant. But what?

Brom. Well, I don't know how to explain, and I'm probably all wrong, but this is supposed to be a democracy.

Stuyvesant. Democracy? What's a democracy?

Brom. It's—it's where you're governed by amateurs. It's a—a free country.

Stuyvesant. Ridiculous.

Vanderbilt. Maybe it vasn't going to be a free country no more—

Brom. Yes, that's what I'm afraid of!

Stuyvesant. Enough! Arrest him!

Poffenburgh. Forward! March!

Brom. Aren't you even going to give me a trial?

Stuyvesant. Trial, hell! When a man's guilty what the hell good's a trial! To jail with him! We'll deal with his case later! Who is the jailer?

Schermerhorn. I am der jailer.

Stuyvesant. If he escapes, shoot the jailer!

Van Cortlandt, Jr. I don't like so many rules.

Roosevelt. Ve used to make the rules.
> [*As the* SOLDIERS *come forward,* BROM *seizes a musket from* SOLDIER *at his right, knocks down four men, and then hears* TINA'S *voice.*]

Tina. Brom! Brom! You promised me!
> [TINA *runs to* BROM'S *side.* BROM *returns musket and submits to arrest. He is led off quickly. The* CROWD *is silent.*]

Stuyvesant. Are these the proper faces for merriment and gaiety? Let me see you smile! Smile. Smile.
> [*The* CROWD *smiles.*]

Now sing. Sing, I say!
> [*He faces* TIENHOVEN *and* THE COUNCIL.]

Sing by the Almighty, or I may forget myself!

Tienhoven.
> [*Weakly*]

        All hail, the political honeymoon—

Stuyvesant. Sing, I say, sing like a man!
> [STUYVESANT *sings.*]

        All hail, the political honeymoon!
> [*A silence*]

Poffenburgh!
> [SOLDIERS *enter.*]

Now sing!

              Tienhoven

> [*Loudly*]

        All hail, the political honeymoon!

Stuyvesant. Now, then, everybody! Because I'm watching you!

The Crowd

All hail the political honeymoon,
    Sing the news to hoi polloi
Of each individual man his boon
    In an age of strength through joy!
Oh, every backward tribe and nation,
Receive this transubstantiation!
    An alchemist sublime
    Transforms our age and time,
       With a twist of the wrist
       This alchemist
    Transforms our age and time!

[*As the* CROWD *sings* STUYVESANT *makes his way among them, exhorting them to enthusiasm. One by one, under the guns, they come to life and the anthem rises to tremendous volume at its close.*]

CURTAIN

KNICKERBOCKER HOLIDAY
ACT TWO

Act Two

SCENE I

*SCENE & & The interior of the jail, a small frame quadrangle
with no furniture save a wooden bench along one wall. There is only
one door—to the right—and no windows. A row of notches, beginning
small at the right, runs around the room, increasing in size, until it
culminates at the left in a gigantic notch, big enough for a man to squeeze
through. It is dark. A book lies open under the candle. Brom is lying back
on the bench, playing his flute softly. Tenpin is sharpening a knife.
Brom drifts into the overture to a ballad that Washington Irving sings.*

Irving

When first men fled from Eden fair
    And spread upon the ground
The honest men were much annoyed
    By thieves that hung around.

They stole the horses from the barns,
    They stole the eggs and hams,
Made inroads on the cattle and
    Among the sheep and lambs.

And so the honest men sat down
    Around a pot of ale
And made a law that all the thieves
    Should be confined in jail,

Whereat the thieves were all confined
    Behind those dismal bars,

So honest men could walk abroad
   To businesses or wars.

But then there was a clever thief
   Who up and said, said he,
The honest men have grown so few,
   So numerous are we,

That if we band together now
   Against the honest men,
The honest men will go to jail
   And we'll go free again.

So then the thieves and robbers rose
   By two's and three's and four's,
And put the honest men away
   Behind those clanging doors.

And since that time it has obtained,
   And will obtain, no doubt,
The honest men sit in the jails—
   The robbers—they are out!

Tenpin. Brom, you should see the Governor out there now. He's got the population lined up like so many suits of winter underwear on a clothes-line. Every time he pulls the string they jump. The council lost four hundred pounds in one afternoon. He'll have these notches plugged up before noon tomorrow.

Brom. It's all rather disturbing, of course, but on the whole I'm inclined to welcome any change after that three-ton congress of imbecility.

   [*A pistol is thrust in through the large notch, followed by* SCHERMER-HORN'S *face.*]

Schermerhorn. Brom Broeck!

Brom. Yes, sir.

Schermerhorn. You vas not supposed to have vomens coming to the chail!

Brom. I know that. But I haven't had any women here.

Schermerhorn. You vill have! Tina Tienhoven has come, and she vants to go in!

Tina.
   [*Outside*]
   Brom!

Brom. Yes, Tina.

Tina.
   [*Looking in*]
   I have to see you to give you back your ring—because I'm to marry another now. Can't you explain to Mynheer Schermerhorn?
   [*She pushes* SCHERMERHORN *aside.*]

Schermerhorn. Quid pushing me.

Tina. Get me in somehow. I must see you.
   [SCHERMERHORN *reappears in notch.*]

Brom. Oh, then she must come in, Mynheer Schermerhorn. It would never do to become engaged to the Governor while wearing another man's ring.

Schermerhorn. No, dot vouldn't do.

Brom. Couldn't you take her round by the door?

Schermerhorn. Oh, no, oh, no! My vife vatches dot door, and she's a derrible voman, my vife. Ve couldn't do dot.

Brom. Couldn't you help her in through the notch, then?

Schermerhorn. It couldn't be ledding people oud ven you led people in, could it?

Brom. Oh, no, that's not the same at all.

Tenpin. No, no!

Schermerhorn. I guess maybe I god to led her in.

Tina. Quick, I haven't much time!

> [*There is a noise at the entrance.*]

Tenpin. Look out—there's someone at the door.

> [TINA *disappears from the notch and* POFFENBURGH *enters followed by* STUYVESANT *and* ROOSEVELT. BROM *and* TENPIN *stand near the wall.*]

Stuyvesant. This is the jail?

Roosevelt. Yes, sir.

Stuyvesant. I hope it's solidly constructed?

Roosevelt. Vell, it used to be pretty good, before it got vittled down.

Stuyvesant.

> [*His eye following the notches*]

Is that a decorative frieze or a ventilating system?

Roosevelt. It's a leak.

Stuyvesant. And is there any reason known to gods or men why the prisoners don't go out through that convenient orifice?

Schermerhorn.

> [*Thrusting in his pistol*]

Because I'm here.

Stuyvesant. Less enthusiasm with that weapon, my friend.

> [*To* TENPIN]

What are you doing here?

Tenpin. I just came in to visit.

Stuyvesant. Throw him out.

Poffenburgh. Yes, sir.

> [*He pushes* TENPIN *through the notch.*]

Stuyvesant.

> [*To* Brom]

> You enjoy it here, I suppose? The food is good, the accommodations satisfactory?

Brom. No, sir.

Stuyvesant. Well, the place appears to be a regular sieve—why haven't you run away?

Brom. I've been occupying myself with philosophical reflections on the nature of government.

Stuyvesant. And what are your conclusions?

Brom. I don't believe you quite understand me, sir. I'm really a very serious and conscientious person. I wouldn't want to escape from jail if I thought I was in the wrong.

Stuyvesant. No? I don't know that I've ever come across that attitude in a felon before, but it's refreshing. A bit naive and provincial, perhaps, but agreeable to the authorities.

Brom. You see, it's a very difficult problem for me. I naturally want to think well of myself in spite of this anarchistic disease you know about. I try to excuse myself in every way I can.— But I always come up against the fact that we have to have a government, and if everybody was like me there couldn't be any government. So I think maybe I deserve to be in jail.

Stuyvesant. Exactly! The perfection of logic!

Brom. But then, on the other hand, you have a disease, too. You want everybody to think as you think and do as you say, and that's even a more dangerous mania than mine. So you ought to be in jail along with me.

Stuyvesant. Oh, I should be in jail with you?

Brom. Yes, sir.

Stuyvesant. Why don't you write a book about it?

Brom. A book?

Stuyvesant. Yes, a book, a long book, with chapters, and footnotes and authorities and references. This is an ideal place for the production of literature, my boy. Thought is free within the walls of this institution. In fact, everything's free, and the mind's at liberty to roam. A lot of great books have been written in prison. Don Quixote and Pilgrim's Progress and the Book of Revelations! Don't waste a moment.

> [*Sings*]
> If you want to be alone with time to think,
> If you want to have a fling with pen and ink,
> If you'd utter meanings cryptic
> In words apocalyptic,
> And in high poetic terms the rotting universe assail,
> Then the very best place for you is jail.
>
> A man is at his happiest sitting in jail
> Where they bring in your victuals in the well-known pail,
> Where they never make a charge and you pay no fee,
> And you don't have to figure on the do-re-mi—
> And you say what you think, for even thought is free
> Along with all varieties of liberty
> So long as you're sitting in jail.
>
> Then you don't have to worry with wrong or right,
> Then you're always certain where you'll sleep at night,
> If your sentiments are shocking
> No one listens while you're talking,
> And breakfast, lunch and dinner-time the beans never fail,
> And the very best place for you is jail.
>
> A man is at his happiest sitting in jail,
> They don't serve turtle, and they don't serve quail,
> But you have no bills to pay on the ultimo,

And never have to add up the mi-re-do,
And you say what you think, for speech and thought are
free
Along with all varieties of liberty
So long as you're sitting in jail.

And so we leave you to your meditations. Good night.

Brom. But I haven't said all I wanted to say—

Stuyvesant. Go right on talking. Good night.
[*He goes out.*]

Brom. But he's not a serious person, at all! He's completely irresponsible!

Roosevelt. Boy, even if I understood von vord of vot you said I vouldn't agree mit you.—Not oud loud.
[*He goes out.*]

Tina.
[*Outside*]
Help me up now!
[*She looks in through the notch.*]
Brom!

Brom. Tina!
[*She starts to climb in.*]

Schermerhorn. Vait a minute! I couldn't do it! I got to haf a official paper!

Tina. Paper! Paper!
[*Brom tears a page out of the book. Tina hands it to Schermerhorn.*]
Here's the paper!

Schermerhorn. Vy didn't you tell me? Now I boost you!
[*Tina rises.*]
Vait a minute! Vait a minute! I don't like dot paper! It ain't a good von! Come oud! Come oud now!

Tina. Brom—he's pulling me out!
  [Brom *seizes her and pulls.*]

Brom. Kick him!

Tina. I am kicking him! What do you think I'm doing?

Schermerhorn. You got to come oud! You got to come oud!

Tina. I will not come out! I'll do exactly as I please! Pull harder! Never mind me!
  [*She screams.*]
  Oh, oh.

Brom. What's the matter?

Tina. I'm afraid my skirt's coming off. Never mind! Pull!

Schermerhorn. Come oud! Come oud!

Tina. Quit giving me orders! If you give me orders I shall do just the opposite! Oh, my skirts are all coming off! Wait, Brom, wait!

Schermerhorn. You got to come oud!

Tina. As long as I live I will never again do as I'm told! Never mind me! Pull!
  [Brom *pulls harder, and she comes free into his arms, minus her skirts, dressed only in her bodice and a pair of decorative Dutch drawers.*]

Brom. Tina! Are you hurt?

Tina. No, only everything goes wrong, everything! Now I've lost my skirts and how can we ever get out of here!

Schermerhorn.
  [*At the notch*]
  Gott in Hefen, vot do I see?

Tina. Go away, then!

Schermerhorn. I petter go avay, so I vouldn't drop dead!

Brom. Mynheer Schermerhorn, will you kindly restore the lady's wardrobe to her? Meanwhile, for your own peace of mind, keeping your face averted?

Schermerhorn.
> [*Dropping skirts inside*]
> Von. Two. Tree. Four. Fife. Six. Is it enough?

Tina. One more.

Schermerhorn. Sefen.

Tina. Hand me my skirts, and I'll explain while I dress. The little green one first.
> [BROM *hands* TINA *the green skirt, which she puts on while talking.*]
> You see, this evening my father ordered me to go upstairs and try on my betrothal costume. Ordered me, you see? And suddenly I understood about you, for the first time. About not being able to take orders. I was furious. I went to my room, and I climbed out the window, and I came straight to the jail! Of course, everybody knows a girl ought to marry as her father tells her; I've always known that. And I was going to do as he told me, only when he ordered me I got so mad I couldn't.

Brom. Maybe it's catching.

Tina. Maybe it is. Anyway, I'm not going to marry Stuyvesant— I'm going to marry you!
> [*Picks up second skirt*]

Brom. Tina! You'll defy your father and the Governor—all for me?

Tina. Yes. I have a plan.
> [*She pulls skirt over her head.*]

Brom. What is it?

Tina. But I must dress.
> [*The door opens, and* MISTRESS SCHERMERHORN *enters with a candle.*]

Mistress Schermerhorn. Oh, excuse me! You vas undressing!

[MISTRESS SCHERMERHORN *turns to go, then comes back.*]

Vas you undressing?

[*She discovers* TINA.]

Tina Tienhoven!

Tina. You see, I was—I was—

Mistress Schermerhorn. Ja, I vas quite sure you vas! Your father shall hear of this instantly! This modern generation! This unspeakable modern generation!

[*She bolts out the door.*]

Brom. Now what?

Tina. Give me the pink one! Hurry!

Brom. But your plan! Your plan! Quick, before she returns!

Tina. It's this! We'll shake the dust of this town from our feet forever! We'll steal a boat, escape from Manhattan and seek out an obscure retreat in the wilderness out beyond Flushing!

Brom. But you've forgotten the Indians. We'd be scalped and murdered in bed on our wedding night, and though, in a way, it might be worth it, still you should ask yourself seriously whether you wish to sacrifice your entire future for one night in my arms.

Tina. Oh.

Brom. Why do you say "Oh"?

Tina. Well, it is a question.

Brom. It is. Because we have a chance under the new Governor, but none with the Indians.

Tina. But you're in jail, after all, and I'm supposed to marry him.

Brom. But if I could get out of jail and you could avoid marrying him, I'd like that better than leading you to your death under the most romantic circumstances.

[*She sighs and turns away.*]

But if you like, we'll go.

Tina. You're not very enthusiastic!
  [*She turns back.*]

Brom. I can't make up my mind whether it's your life alone that I don't like to endanger, or whether I'm also somewhat concerned about my own.

Tina. Does a man think about such things?

Brom. Unless he's a complete damn fool he devotes some attention to his prospects of survival, yes!

Tina. And here I was, thinking how tragically beautiful it would be.
  [*Looks up, then out toward audience*]
  We'd be figures in story, the legendary lovers of the early Dutch occupation, Brom and Tina, drinking passion and death together in one dark draught!

Brom. I'd love to read about it, but that pleasure, unfortunately, would never be mine!

Tina. You're right, of course.

Brom. Oh, yes, I'm right.

Tina. And the only sensible thing is to leave you here—
  [*Moves away to left*]
  return to my father's house, and make myself ready to sleep with old Silverleg, who is probably a very good sort of fellow, though he smells horribly of snuff.

Brom. How do you know?

Tina. I'm afraid I know him better than you do. He kissed me.

Brom. Kissed you?
  [*Crosses toward her*]
  More than once?

Tina. Oh, a number of times, rather embarrassingly.

Brom. Not with passion?

Tina. For an old man he was far from listless. What's more, it's all arranged that I'm to marry him tomorrow.

Brom. Tomorrow! Tomorrow! Come, we will go! We'll surmount every obstacle, and make our escape tonight!

[*He starts toward notch, pulling her.*]

Tina.

[*Stops him*]

We'll be shot down in our early twenties, you know, and time will end for us at that moment!

Brom. Then let one arrow transfix both hearts together, two hearts that cannot be divided!

[*He pulls again.*]

Tina.

[*She holds him.*]

If I married the Governor I'd probably live quite safely to the age of ninety, have ten children by him, and hundreds of grand-children!

Brom. Bother his grandchildren! Come, let us die quickly together, while we're still young and hopeful and wildly in love!

Tina. There, that's exactly what I wanted you to say!

[*They kiss.*]

Brom. Then for God's sake hurry with those skirts! Must you put them all on before we escape?

Tina.

[*She whirls up to him.*]

Brom, would you have me seen in the streets without all my skirts on?

Brom. Certainly!

Tina. You're right! Let them keep my skirts as souvenirs of the first grand passion on the American continent! Come!

Brom. Come, Tina!

[*As they rush to the notch an iron grating is clapped over the opening, and* SCHERMERHORN *fastens it into place.*]

Schermerhorn. Der Governor says now we pud iron bars across so ve could haf somebody to hang!

Brom. Too late!

Tina. And that's the end of my rebellion! Oh, is there never any such thing as beauty or good fortune or high romance? You set out with such great hopes, such gallant aspirations, and you end up in jail—practically undressed!

Brom. My fault!

Tina. No, mine!

[*They kiss.*]

Schermerhorn. Maybe you petter kiss good because you vouldn't live so long as you tink.

[*The door opens and* TIENHOVEN *enters with* ROOSEVELT *and* MISTRESS SCHERMERHORN. *The* MARSHAL *pokes his pistol in.*]

Tienhoven. You vas a huzzy!

Tina. Oh, no, father.

Tienhoven. Pud on your ouder skirt, and come with me.

Tina. Where are we going?

[*Backs behind* BROM]

Tienhoven. All dis got to be hushed up, because you got to marry der Governor.

Tina. I'm going to marry Brom! I shall tell the Governor that I don't love him, and my affections are elsewhere engaged!

Tienhoven. No, you von't. Because if you said one vord about dot I fix it mit der Governor so Brom hangs tomorrow for der betrothal celebration.

Tina. But father! He wouldn't hang the man I love at my betrothal!

Tienhoven. He vouldn't? Der got to be a government, and it got to hang people. Come on.

[*He drags* TINA *out with him.*]

Brom

[*Sitting on the bench, sings*]

Oh, life and love are a series of separations
Resembling all too closely vivisection,
A mingled yarn of infinite alternations
With now and then one moment of perfection.

[TINA *returns to the door and sings with* BROM *through the bars.*]

Tina and Brom

We are cut in twain who would be one flesh
And naturally we bleed;
The tears flow fast for the wound is fresh
And desperate our need.

Tina

Life seems to me but a series of obligations
Like notes of hand presented for collection,
Or mortgages foreclosed by our near relations
To cancel, void and nullify affection.

Tina and Brom

We are cut in twain who would be one flesh
And naturally we bleed;
The tears flow fast for the wound is fresh
And desperate our need.

Brom

Oh, life and love are compact of mortifications,
    The curbs of age upon youth's predilection;
Youth swears its love upon the constellations,
    Age holds the stars are subject to correction.

Tina and Brom

We are cut in twain who would be one flesh
    And naturally we bleed;
The tears flow fast for the wound is fresh
    And desperate our need.

[TIENHOVEN *drags* TINA *away*.]

CURTAIN

Prologue to Act Two

SCENE II

Irving

[*Sings*]
Winners lose
    And losers win,
Put your money down and watch
    The planet spin.
All good fortune changes hands
    Inevitably,
And the fish you couldn't catch are
    Still in the sea.

When your hat lets rain in because it has no crown,
    And your feet are wet and getting wetter,
When you're on rock bottom, and you can't go down,
    Any change is for the better.
When your luck bows out, and you go to jail,
    And you're on the inside looking out at the cop,
When your friends say sorry, and you can't get bail,
    Then there's nowhere to go but up.
To the man who has aplenty
    Any change is for the worse
So he plays a losing hand
    Against the universe,
But in wintry weather, when the leaves turn brown,
    And the banker has a mortgage on your crop,
When you're on rock bottom, and you can't go down,
    Then there's nowhere to go but up!

Act Two

*SCENE   &   &   The scene is again the Battery as seen from the
waterfront. It is the morning of the day following Scene I.
As the Curtain rises we discover* STUYVESANT *seated at left stage at a small
table, eating and drinking heartily. A* SOLDIER *is kneeling at his right pol-
ishing* STUYVESANT'S *silver leg. As the curtain reaches its full opening the*
GRAND ARMY *of New Amsterdam marches in from up right. The*
ARMY *consists of* THE COUNCIL, CORLEAR, SIX BOYS *and are com-
manded by* GENERAL POFFENBURGH. VAN CORTLANDT, JR. *leads the*
ARMY *bearing a standard, which displays the colors of New Amsterdam.
He is followed by the* SIX BOYS *in double file, and behind them,* THE
COUNCIL *and* CORLEAR *also in double file.* GENERAL POFFENBURGH
*stands on the top platform just below the gallows giving commands.
The* ARMY *marches to left stage above the gallows, makes a right face
and marches down the steps and marches until* VAN CORTLANDT, JR.
reaches the extreme right stage.

Poffenburgh. Army, halt, one two! Right face!

   [*They obey.*]

Sir, the Army of New Amsterdam!

Stuyvesant. At ease!

   [*They obey.*]

I have but one fault to find with this army! There is still too
much individual thinking in the ranks! Take care! Individual
thinking can be detected without the slightest difficulty by any
good officer! It shows in every movement, in the response to
every order. You, sir, Roosevelt!

   [ROOSEVELT *has seated himself comfortably on the steps at left.*]

It shows in your face at this moment!

   [ROOSEVELT *stands in line again.*]

What are you thinking?

   [ROOSEVELT *comes down to* STUYVESANT'S *right.*]

Roosevelt. Excuse me. I was tinking, I don't like to be pushed
around. And anyvay, vot's der good of marching in a army ven
ve vasn't fighting nobody?

Stuyvesant. My dear sir, my nature is so irritable, my temper so uncertain, my habit of mind so pugnacious, that we shall be at war very shortly, very shortly.

Roosevelt. Dot's awful.

Stuyvesant. On the contrary, it's a therapeutic measure. A nation at peace grows fat-headed and short-winded—as witness your own mental and physical condition. A short war with say— Connecticut, preferably victorious, would restore tone. Why, the Connecticans have built a fort on the Connecticut River, within our territories, and they must, of course, be driven out, whatever the cost in patriot blood!

Vanderbilt. Den ve get in a war!

Stuyvesant. Naturally.

Tienhoven. Mit all of Connecticut! Dot's awful!

The Council. Derrible!

Roosevelt. Couldn't ve send dem a letter? Maybe ve could make a deal and give dem Boston.

Stuyvesant. That is exactly the spirit which I intend to destroy among you! You have grown fat and foolish for lack of an antagonist! Since we have no enemies it is necessary to create them! You sir, Tienhoven, why aren't you holding your head up?

Tienhoven. Der is von question I could maybe vant to ask?

Stuyvesant. What is it?

Tienhoven. Ven ve march up to der fort is it absolutely necessary I should march in front?

Stuyvesant. An intelligent question, Mynheer Tienhoven. Allow me to answer you by a brief demonstration of military tactics. Company, attention! Left face!

[The ARMY *wheels so that its members face left stage.* STUYVESANT *moves to the front of the formation.* THE COUNCIL *is behind him and the* BOYS *are at the rear.]*

We are now, my men, in parade formation, with the gravest, wisest, most eloquent, most dignified of our citizens in the front rank. This, in all civilized countries, is the proper order for parades and other civil functions. About face!

[The ARMY *obeys. We now find the* BOYS *lead the formation,* THE COUNCIL *next, and* STUYVESANT *is in the rear, well protected.]*

This, on the other hand, is military formation for field duty and attack. The youngest and most active in the front, the older and more valuable in the rear!

[To TIENHOVEN]

Does that answer your question?

Tienhoven. Absolutely.

Stuyvesant. Poffenburgh! Maneuvers! Hold your heads erect for I shall be watching you!

*[*GENERAL POFFENBURGH *puts the* ARMY *through complicated drilling, and the* ARMY *sings the War Song as it drills.]*

The Army

To war, to war, to war!
We don't want what we are fighting for!
To war, to war, to war!
But that's all right when soldiers go to war.

Oh, if we leave the maidens we adore,
It's not exactly that we fancy more,
To come home feet first, laid out six by four,
Or minus parts the surgeon can't restore,
Or that we've been offered gold,
No it's only that we're told:
To war, to war, to war!
To war, to war, to war!

Oh, if we leave our homes and go to fight,
It's not because we're certain that we're right,
Or even that it fills us with delight
That we'll be slaughtered heroes by tonight,
Or that we mind growing old,
No, it's only that we're told:
To war, to war, to war!
To war, to war, to war!

[STUYVESANT *marches across in front of the* ARMY *and back again, displaying great vigour.*]

Stuyvesant. No! More spirit—more spirit! Watch me!

[*He walks in front of* ARMY *to right. Turns and crosses back. Sees* ARMY *imitating his peg leg.*]

That's more like it!

[*He sits.*]

And now, General Poffenburgh, there is to be a brief meeting of the council before the review. The council members will fall out and remain with me, the others will return with you for further drill.

[POFFENBURGH *salutes.*]

Poffenburgh. Attention! Council fall out! Army right face! Forward march!

[*The* ARMY *marches out, leaving* STUYVESANT *and* THE COUNCIL. *The* GOVERNOR *seats himself and* THE COUNCIL *sits with him.*]

Stuyvesant. First of all, there appears to be a slight misunderstanding about our fiscal system. I announced that prices, profits and wages were to be doubled. Why has it not been done?

[*A silence*]

de Vries. How could ve do it?

Stuyvesant. By doubling them. Is that plain?

de Vries. Ja, dot's plain. Vich von doubles first?

Stuyvesant. First we raise wages. That necessitates a rise in prices, which naturally brings about a rise in profits. Is that plain?

de Vries. Ja, dot's pretty plain. Couldn't ve just raise profits but not vages?

Stuyvesant. What do you think?

de Vries. Ja, dot's plain, too.

de Peyster. Maybe ve raise prices so high nobody buys anyting?

Stuyvesant. In that case it might be necessary to reduce prices.

de Peyster. Vages, too?

Stuyvesant. Wages, however, we shall never reduce. A reduction in wages would have a most unfortunate effect on my following.

Tienhoven. But suppose prices goes down, how could vages stay up?

Stuyvesant. They must and will stay up. I shall see that they do.

de Vries. Dere goes my sausage business!

Van Rensselaer. I'm a ruined man!

Everyone. Ruined!

Stuyvesant. My dear fellows, you speak in the terms of an outworn economy. Under my system there is no such thing as ruin, and no such thing as bankruptcy; there is only a slight financial sophistication supported by unlimited government credit.

Van Rensselaer. Ah!

The Council. Ah!

Tienhoven. Der government vill gif credit?

Stuyvesant. Unlimited credit.

Roosevelt. To anybody, py golly?

Stuyvesant. To absolutely anybody.

Roosevelt. Der must be a ketch in it.

Stuyvesant. There is. The government will naturally become a partner in any business which it guarantees.

Vanderbilt. A silent partner, mebbe?

Stuyvesant. Quite conversational.

Vanderbilt. Taxes vould be high, yes?

Stuyvesant. Taxes will be moderately high, yes.

de Peyster. But may be ve couldn't pay dem high taxes and high vages, so nobody vorks, so nobody buys anyting, so nobody makes any profit, so it stops going!

Stuyvesant. It might happen.
> [*He smiles.*]

In that case the government would have to take over.

Council. Oh!

de Vries. Maybe ve all gonto be sophisticated?

Stuyvesant. It's possible.

de Vries. Maybe der government gonto own everyting?

Stuyvesant. It's possible.
> [*He rises.*]

de Vries. Maybe von man gonto run der whole vorks?

Stuyvesant. It's possible.—And now, perhaps we understand each
other.—Not that it matters.

[*Walks left and out;* THE COUNCIL *look at each other sadly.*]

de Vries. It's like Julius Caesar, dot Italian.

Vanderbilt. It's like Attila, dot Aryan.

Roosevelt. Now, vere ve got our ancient liberties?

[THE COUNCIL *draws together, shaking heads sorrowfully.*]

The Council

[*Sings*]

Ja, vere ve got our ancient liberties?
From back before Columbus,
As far as Pericles,
A Dutchman was a free man,
And vould not bend his knees;
From Spanisher to Britisher
Ve put der tyrants down,
And never vas a Hollander
Vot feared a kingly frown—
Now vere ve got our ancient liberties?

Ja, vere ve got our ancient liberties?
Since Adam in der garden
Vas eating off der trees
A Dutchman keeps his neck up
To do as he vould please;
Now gomes anoder Dutchman in,
A slicker from der town,

And fetches us mit promises
    To lay dot freedom down—
Now vere ve got our ancient liberties?

Ja, vere ve got our ancient liberties?
    Von time a man at vorking
        Took comfort in his soul,
He took his long pipe in his hand
    Ven he vent forth to bowl,
And wheresoe'er his eye was cast .
    Across der lands or seas
A Dutchman vas a citizen
    And he could take his ease—
Now vere ve got our ancient liberties?

[THE COUNCIL *exits to the right very slowly. The lights dim out to show the passage of time, and come up a moment later as a night scene.* SIX GIRLS *enter from up left, costumed for the betrothal ceremony. As they sing* TINA *enters from her house.*]

The Girls

Behold the fates and years contrary
Plighting May and January,
Behold sweet sixteen, pale as ashes,
Shrinking from his gray mustaches,
Behold the little flower, love-crossed,
Trembling at the touch of frost—

[*The* SIX BOYS *enter from up right carrying lanterns.* VAN CORT-LANDT, JR. *enters with betrothal papers, crosses to center and stands waiting for* TINA'S *and* STUYVESANT'S *signatures. The lights slowly build to full.*]

⬚ 88 ⬚

The Chorus

Behold the maid with blushes cherry
Gives her hand where she will marry;
Behold the spring with winter crosses,
Equalizing solar losses;
Behold the rainbow bridge of mirth
Joins this paradise with earth—
Joins heaven with earth!
Joins youth and ancient cheer!
Joins love and worth,
Romance and musketeer!

[THE COUNCIL *enters from down right,* MARSHAL SCHERMERHORN *and his* WIFE *enter from down left, then* STUYVESANT *enters from the house and crosses to* TINA *at center, who is signing her name in the betrothal book, which is held by* VAN CORTLANDT, JR.]

Stuyvesant. My dear, have you memorized the little handful of rules which I drew up for the guidance of the wives of New Amsterdam?

Tina. I'm afraid—not all of them.

Stuyvesant. Then put on your thinking cap, my dear, for you will need those precepts before nightfall.

Tina. Governor Stuyvesant!

Stuyvesant. Yes?

Tina. I—No, I can't ask him. I don't dare.

Stuyvesant. Tut—what was the very first admonition on your list, child? Repeat them all, from the beginning.

Tina. Rules for the wives of New Amsterdam—

Stuyvesant. One.

Tina. One. A wife should have nothing on her mind which she does not tell her husband, and should tell her husband nothing which does not give him pleasure.

Stuyvesant. Quite accurate. Two.

Tina. Two. Husband and wife should never pass in the doorway. She should never go out as he comes in, nor come in as he goes out.

Stuyvesant. And, as a corollary, the less she goes out the better. Three.

Tina. Three. She shall avoid all demonstrations of affection except when alone with her husband, for a Hollander's lady, like Caesar's wife, must be beyond reproach.

Stuyvesant. A crude rule, but necessary. Four.

Tina. Four. No dinner is good unless hot.

Stuyvesant. Ah, there is the heart of domestic science! Never forget that rule!

Tina. Five. For breakfast the wife should provide a great number of fresh eggs which have been boiled three minutes by the glass, and a great rasher of bacon, neatly fried, and she should smile constantly at her husband across these eggs and bacon, for a man is never at his best in the morning, and needs encouragement.—I never can do it!—Never!

Stuyvesant. You will do extremely well at first, and better later, my dear, for as a woman loses her charms she begins to excel in cookery.
    [*Starts to sign the betrothal book*]
Can anyone give reason why this troth should not be plighted?

Mistress Schermerhorn. I can!

Stuyvesant. What?

The Crowd. What!

Stuyvesant. What reason?

Mistress Schermerhorn. She visited the jail last night in a most indelicate and indecent manner!

Stuyvesant. This sweet and innocent girl?

Mistress Schermerhorn. She's not so innocent!

Stuyvesant.
[*Turning to* TINA]
Did you visit the jail last night?

Tina. Yes, sir.

Stuyvesant. For what purpose?

Tina. To return Brom's ring to him.

Stuyvesant. You were engaged to Brom Broeck?

Tina. Yes, sir.

Stuyvesant. You went to the jail to break the engagement and return his ring?

Tina. Yes, sir.

Stuyvesant. Why, a perfectly sound and moral reason.

Mistress Schermerhorn. Then why did she kiss him?

Stuyvesant.
[*Wincing*]
Did you—ah—kiss him?

Tina. I kissed him farewell.

Stuyvesant. Quite proper. Quite proper. I don't say that the young gentleman may not regret that kiss in the future, but your conduct was justifiable.

Mistress Schermerhorn. Then why did she take her skirts off?

Stuyvesant.
[*Taking* TINA *by hand and leading her down center.*]
Did you—ah—take your skirts off?

⚜ 91 ⚜

120930

Tina.
> [*Defiantly*]
> No.

Mistress Schermerhorn. But they were off! She can't deny that!

Stuyvesant. Were they—ah—off?

Tina. Yes.

Stuyvesant. You make matters very difficult for me. How did this happen?

Tina. Marshal Schermerhorn pulled them off.

Schermerhorn. Only in the discharge of my official duties, Your Excellency.

Stuyvesant. And now am I to believe it's within the province of a jailer to remove the skirts of lady visitors?

Schermerhorn. She climbs trough der hole mitout a permit, so I pull back on her, but she comes apart!

Stuyvesant. Is this the true story of what happened?

Tina. Yes, sir.

Stuyvesant. And you are still technically a maiden?

Tina. Yes, sir.

Stuyvesant. Then we erase the whole episode. It is not be expected that a maiden arrives at a marriageable age without sundry contacts of one kind and another which it would be just as well not to discuss in public.
> [*He sings.*]

When a military man is at the height of his career
And marching his battalion off to wars,
He's fought numerous engagements for his country far
                    and near
In serving his apprenticeship to Mars.
        And he naturally accumulates some decorative scars
        In serving his apprenticeship to Mars.

Chorus

        And he naturally accumulates some decorative scars
        In serving his apprenticeship to Mars.

Stuyvesant

Now a melting maiden's marriage is the height of her
                    career
And unless she is particularly stupid
She's fought many a minor battle for her country
                    front and rear
In serving her apprenticeship to Cupid.
        And she naturally accumulates experimental scars
        In winning these preliminary wars.

Chorus

        And she naturally accumulates experimental scars
        In winning these preliminary wars.

Stuyvesant

When a soldier takes a maiden and a maiden takes a man
For free exchange of philogenic blisses,
Let both of them remember, as a part of Nature's plan,
It's practice that makes perfect in our kisses.
        When lovely Venus lies beside her lord and master
                    Mars
        They mutually profit by their scars.

[STUYVESANT *and* TINA *dance a short minuet and everyone else follows their example. Then* STUYVESANT *breaks into a fast dance with the* GIRLS *of the* CROWD. *This is broken by the sounds of shots, men yelling and all the noises of battle. In the middle of this noise,* BROM *and* TENPIN *enter up left at a run.*]

Stuyvesant. Is he out again?

Brom. The Indians burned down the jail! Drunken Indians! We're all dead men! Run for your lives!

[*The* CROWD *starts off right in a mad scramble, as the noise increases.* BROM *starts off and* TINA *calls to him, trying to catch up to him.*]

Tina. Brom! Wait for me!

[*They run out together.*]

[*The stage is now empty except for* STUYVESANT. TIENHOVEN *enters from up left, running.*]

Tienhoven. We've been betrayed! Run for your lives!

Stuyvesant. Rally the Grand Army!

Tienhoven. You rally the Grand Army!

[*He runs out right.*]

[STUYVESANT *is now alone on the stage again. Indian war whoops approach and a band of* INDIANS *burst upon the scene.* STUYVESANT *runs out to the others as the* INDIANS *do a war dance. When they have finished they run out down left.* STUYVESANT *appears immediately down right, urging his* ARMY *forward.*]

Stuyvesant. Come, soldiers of the Grand Army. Fall in and we'll send these Algonquins hopping back to Harlem! Forward!

The Army. To war, to war, to war! We don't want—

[*The* INDIANS *break in again. The* COUNCILMEN *fall over each other trying to escape.* ROOSEVELT *hides behind* STUYVESANT, *who stands fearless. The* INDIANS *run out as soon as they are in.* STUYVESANT *starts to urge the* ARMY *forward again.*]

Stuyvesant. Rally, my men! Rally in the open! Don't get behind me! Must I face them alone! Forward!

[*They start forward once more.*]

The Army. To war, to war, to war! We don't want—

[*The* INDIANS *run in again.* BROM *and* TENPIN *have entered at the rear of* THE COUNCIL. *Everyone ducks his head, ostrich-fashion, with his posterior towards the audience.*]

Stuyvesant. You block-headed sons of a degenerate race! File into the block-house then, and we'll at least defend ourselves!

[THE COUNCIL *dashes into the fort.* BROM *and* TENPIN *turn and start out right, the way they entered.*]

Into the block-house! Get in, you apostle of panic, you runner-away from Indians!

Brom.
[*Turning*]
Me?

Stuyvesant. Yes, you! Get inside with the others! You can at least handle a musket!

Brom.
[*Advancing on* STUYVESANT]
You're giving me an order! You're ordering me not to fight the Indians?

Stuyvesant. I am! Get inside! Both of you!

Brom.
[*Moves toward* STUYVESANT *threateningly*]
You tin-pot military man! Get inside yourself! Come on, Tenpin, after those Indians!

[BROM *and* TENPIN *start out up left. An* INDIAN *runs in at* BROM. *He picks* INDIAN *up and hurls him offstage. They exit.* TINA *runs in from down right. She runs up steps at right and crosses to below gallows.*]

Tina. Brom! Brom! Come back!

Stuyvesant.
[*Laughing*]
You've seen the last of him!
[*There is a crash off stage.*]

Tina. Oh, oh! He's knocked the chief down!

[*Three crashes—*STUYVESANT *turns toward the battle in astonishment.*]

Oh, what a fighter—what a man in battle!

[*As she ducks, an arrow strikes the gallows over her head, quivering. As* STUYVESANT *steps backward upstage, an arrow strikes the platform of the gallows by his leg. There are tremendous battle noises off left.*]

Stuyvesant. Let us go to his assistance! Does anyone follow me?

[*He turns to* THE COUNCIL. *No one anwers.*]

Faint hearts! Then I go alone!

[*He seizes a musket and stumps out left. As he does so, an* INDIAN *approaches.* STUYVESANT *kicks the* INDIAN *out with his silver leg. A tremendous cheer goes up from all.*]

Schermerhorn.

[*Coming out of the fort*]

Py Criminy, I go myself, mebbe!

[*As he crosses, a shot is heard just off left. He turns hastily and goes out down right as he speaks.*]

Vere's my vife? Better I should ask my vife!

[*An arrow hits him in the rear. There are more battle sounds and cries.*]

Vanderbilt. Look at Brom!

Van Rensselaer. Look at Stuyvesant!

Tienhoven. It's peautiful! Peautiful!

[*As* TIENHOVEN *speaks, an arrow hits the fort by his head and he jumps in fright.*]

The Crowd.

[*Cheering*]

Brom Broeck! Stuyvesant! Stuyvesant! Brom Broeck!

Corlear. The Governor's down! Stuyvesant's fallen! Now Tenpin's fallen! Now Brom's down!

Tina. They're killing him! I can look no more!

Roosevelt.

> [*Moving to left of gallows*]

Look! Brom got up again! He got up and he looks bigger as a giant! Wham! Now he starts vonce more! Nefer vas anyting like dot in der history of New Amsterdam! Swash! Oh, vot a good von! Oh, vot a good von! He saves der Governor! Der Governor fights again! Ve vin!

Tienhoven. Make der announcement!

Corlear. Stuyvesant and Brom, the winners!

> [*The* CROWD *cheers.*]

Schermerhorn.

> [*Entering*]

Dey vin! Now ve all gotta help!

> [*The* BOYS *run in from down right and go out up left.* SCHERMERHORN *follows them at a careful distance.* THE COUNCIL *move left toward the battle, all of them leaving the fort. The* GIRLS *run in from down right. They all cheer as they advance. Then suddenly the cheering stops and* TINA *gasps.*]

Tina. Oh!

1st Girl.

> [*Moving up steps left*]

Who is it? Somebody's been killed.

> ["*The Dirge*" *is heard off left.*]

1st Girl. They're carrying Tenpin!

2nd Girl. Tenpin's been killed!

1st Girl. Poor fellow!

The Chorus

[*Sings*]

Drawn to the earth
The soldier lies,
With beat of drum we usher him home.
Emptied of mirth
His blinded eyes
Stare at the grass-roots whence we come.

[Boys *enter from up left*, Two Soldiers *carrying* Tenpin *on a stretcher. They form a funeral procession. As they sing, they march down the steps at left. The* Soldiers *lay* Tenpin *below the step at center.*]

Roll, roll the drum for a soldier,
Grieve, grieve for the heart of dust,
Mourn, mourn, for there lives none bolder,
Weep, weep for the bright blade's rust.

Sighing, sighing,
For a soldier's dying,
Wake the hills' replying,
Still the wild heart's crying,
Turn, and leave him where he's lying!

Back to the ground
The soldier goes,
No toll of bell for his last farewell,
But a trumpet's sound
In the grave-yard close
Hallows the plot where he shall dwell!

Roll, roll the drum for a soldier,
Grieve, grieve for the heart of dust,
Mourn, mourn, for there lives none bolder,
Weep, weep for the bright blade's rust.

[Stuyvesant *and* Brom *enter from the battle.*]

Stuyvesant. Young man, much as I dislike to admit it, you have saved my life, and your disobedience has saved the honor of the city.

I cannot pardon you, naturally. You will have to stand trial for impertinent disregard of a military order, but you have earned the right to speak the last words over your comrade, fallen in battle. Tenpin's fellow soldier shall speak for him now.

Brom. I'd better not say anything.

Stuyvesant. It's fitting that you should.

Tina.
> [*Coming down the steps at left*]
> Yes, Brom. Speak a word over Tenpin.

Brom. I'd better not. You see, I've lost a dear friend, and I've been hit over the head, and between the two I'm thinking much too clearly to be sane.

A Boy. Speak up, Brom! Climb up a little, so we can see you!

Stuyvesant. Make a place for him!

Brom. This ceremony's quite meaningless, because nobody really liked him except me, and he can't hear us anyway. The truth about a dead soldier is usually that he died young, in an unnecessary war, because of the stupidity or ambition of those in office. It was so in this case. That's the whole truth about the death of poor old Tenpin.

Stuyvesant. May I remind you that a certain regard for the feelings of the existing government is customary even in funeral addresses?

Brom. I confess that I had certain illusions about the existing government when it first arrived. But today as Tenpin and I sat in jail we saw a tribe of Indians purchasing firearms and firewater from the ship. The implements of war with which they carried out this last attack were sold to the Indians by Governor Stuyvesant.

Stuyvesant. Citizens, let me call your attention to the fact that this man is already under indictment, and that he makes an unsup-ported charge against my administration! He alone makes this accusation! There is no other witness! Let him bring one wit-ness! One witness besides himself!

[*There is a pause.*]

Tenpin. I'm a witness! I saw it, too! I saw it, too!
[*He rises and stands at* STUYVESANT'S *right.*]
They bought muskets from your ship!

Brom. Tenpin! Tenpin! And now the dead rise to testify against you!

Stuyvesant. This Tenpin fellow is completely unreliable, even when he's dead!

Brom. Gentlemen, this Governor Stuyvesant is obviously a tyrant, but we thought at least he was honest!

Stuyvesant. Young man, once my temper is up, there may occur some deaths which are more or less permanent!

Brom. Governor Stuyvesant, my temper is none too reliable. But shall we confine ourselves to parliamentary procedure for a moment?

Stuyvesant. I offered you my friendship once. I offer it again.

Brom. Last night in jail I got thinking about that ridiculous council of ours you shoved into the background when you came in. You said it was stupid, and it was. It was so inefficient and witless that we could get away with a little fun once in a while. I guess all governments are crooked, I guess they're all vicious and corrupt, but a democracy has the immense advantage of being incompetent in villainy and clumsy in corruption. Now, your tyranny's another matter—

Poffenburgh. Treason! This is treason!

Stuyvesant. Wait! Let him continue.

Brom.

[*To the* CROWD]

I say his tyranny's another matter. It's efficiently vicious and efficiently corrupt! They're both bad. But since we have to have one or the other let's throw out this professional and go back to the rotation of amateurs! Let's keep the government small and funny, and maybe it'll give us less discipline and more entertainment!

Stuyvesant. It sounds as if you were trying to erect your private and personal disease into a public policy! The same city won't hold both of us! General Poffenburgh, the rope, and this time under the left ear!

Brom. You might at least give me an order, and then we could settle the whole thing by personal combat.

Stuyvesant. Is that the best you can do, an invitation to personal combat? It's unworthy of a man with your reputation for cheating the gallows by sleight of hand.

Brom. I've been very fortunate.

Stuyvesant. Oh, very fortunate—I shall never forget how cleverly you tricked the poor old council here! But out-think me! Try your witty strategems on old Pieter Stuyvesant and see how far you get with that!

Brom. Will you give me a minute to think?

Stuyvesant. I'll give you three seconds.

Tina. Governor Stuyvesant!

Stuyvesant. Let him have his three seconds!

Tina. I must warn you of a complication!

Stuyvesant. Another time, another time.

Tina. You must not hang this man!

Stuyvesant. And why not?

Tina. Because—you would not want it said of you that your child was the son of a man who was hanged!

Stuyvesant. Unless I were hanged myself that could hardly be said of me.

Tina. But isn't it true that after we are married any child born to me is legally yours?

Stuyvesant. And actually, I should hope! Actually also! What do you mean?

Tina. I lied about what happened in the jail! It wasn't only kissing! I must confess to a consummated intimacy!

Stuyvesant. Indeed.

Tina. Yes, sir.

Stuyvesant. My child, when you are older and more experienced in lying, you will blush less easily. And if this is an expedient to save your lover, it's not calculated to work that way, I assure you, and you'd better leave all the trickery to him.

Tina. You can't pardon him because of his unborn child?
[*She kneels.*]

Stuyvesant. Whose unborn child? I take no stock in this story of an unborn child! If I believed it I'd hang you both higher than Haman!

Tina. You would? You'd hang us both! Then I'm guilty! In the highest degree! Oh, Brom! It might have been at midnight, it may be at high noon, but whenever death comes it must come to us together!

Brom. Don't interrupt me. I'm trying to think something out.

Tina.
[*To* STUYVESANT]
But you will hang us together?

Stuyvesant. No, but you shall certainly have a front seat at his hanging!

[*To* CORLEAR]

Make the announcement!

Corlear. Oyez, oyez, the final hanging of Brom Broeck! Brom Broeck will absolutely be hanged!

[POFFENBURGH *takes* BROM *up left steps to gallows.* SOLDIERS *shove* BOYS *and* GIRLS *up left.*]

Stuyvesant. General Poffenburgh, proceed with the execution. Mynheer Tienhoven, the council will have the honor of hoisting this rascal into eternity! Range yourselves along the rope! Unless the criminal has thought of a trick to evade his destiny.

Brom. As a matter of fact, I've thought of something better than a trick!

Stuyvesant. Then use it—use it!

Tina. I want to kiss him good-bye!

Stuyvesant. If she wishes to demean herself, let her kiss him.

[*The lovers kiss.*]

Brom. I guess it is good-bye this time, Tina.

Stuyvesant. I think it is, indeed. Because you are at the end of your rope, in more ways than one, my foxy young friend, and nothing will save you now.

Brom. You may be right, but I'd like to say one word to the council. Gentlemen, I used to think there was something wrong with me because I couldn't take orders—but now I know it was a virtue—and one you'd all better learn if you want to live!

Stuyvesant. Cut that speech short! Cut it short!

Brom. I'm sentenced for saying that your government was better than his, and now if you don't want him to hang you all, one by one, you'll throw down that rope and speak up to him!

Stuyvesant. Take in the slack! Up with him! No hesitation!

Tienhoven. Ve petter pull! Come on!

Brom. Does he do your thinking for you, or have you minds of your own!

    [*There is a pause.*]

Roosevelt. No, ve vouldn't pull!

    [*Drops rope*]

Stuyvesant. What?

Roosevelt. Ve vouldn't pull! My name's Roosevelt and ven I get a idea it sticks! Ve vouldn't pull!

Stuyvesant. Will you let him outwit you again?

The Council

[*Sings*]

No, ve vouldn't gonto do it;
No,ve von't hang Brom;
Ve vant our ancient liberties;
Ve gonto make der laws!

The Crowd

[*Sings*]

They aren't going to do it;
They won't hang Brom!
We want our ancient liberties!
We want to make the laws!

Stuyvesant. Has this spirit infected you all! Lean on that rope, or I may find it necessary to purge the commonwealth of recalcitrants!

de Peyster. You sold guns to Indians yourself!

Van Rensselaer. Ja—yourself you did it!

The Crowd. Hurrah for Brom and the council!

Stuyvesant. If it comes to open rebellion the arms are on my side, gentlemen, and I shall use them. Poffenburgh, get ready to fire on the crowd! Will you hang that man or not?

The Council and the Crowd. No!

Roosevelt. More den dot, der council gonto make der laws!

Tienhoven. You better say someting a little bit bleasant, Governor Stuyvesant!

Stuyvesant. Never! I tolerate no opposition! You shall learn the difference between amateurs and professionals, and a bloody lesson it will be! Get ready to fire!

> [POFFENBURGH *wheels a cannon in and hands the lighted taper to* STUYVESANT.]

Irving. I'm sorry to interrupt again but I must have a word with you, Governor Stuyvesant—

Stuyvesant. Who are you?

Irving. I'm Washington Irving, the author.

Stuyvesant. Damn all authors and damn all meddlers! Stay out of this and let me govern my people in my own way!

Irving. Unfortunately, I can't. But in your own interest—quite in your own interest—you should make your peace with the citizens of New Amsterdam! You are, sir, as you know, the patron saint of this city—

Stuyvesant. I wasn't aware that I had reached the stage of desuetude proper for canonization.

Irving. Oh Lord, sir, you died long ago, and your venerated bones and your silver leg still rest in your old chapel, St. Mark's-in-the-Bouerie.

Stuyvesant. This is hardly the moment for mortuary reminiscences. I have a rebellion on my hands here.

Irving. But that's my reason for bringing the matter up. You wouldn't want it said of you, as you lie in your modest tomb, that you destroyed the institutions of a free people because you were intolerant of legitimate opposition. My generation views you with mixed emotions, like every other public man, but rather affectionately on the whole. This bloody step which you contemplate would alter our opinion of you.

Stuyvesant. Tell them to set down with the rest that I enforced discipline, even when I found it disagreeable. Be ready with your flints!

Irving. This is an action, sir, which you would not wish posterity to witness. And you stand now in full view of posterity, lit very brightly and quite conspicuous.

Stuyvesant. I fail to see it.

Irving. Look out beyond the circle of lights, out toward the gleam in the darkness that might be starched linen. Posterity sits in judgment on you in that penumbra of receding faces.

Stuyvesant. Is that posterity—out there?

Irving. Largely Dutch too. The Hollanders were the most prolific and the hardest to kill of all the early settlers.

Stuyvesant. They look a little dim, but I suppose people get that way on ahead in the future. How did they turn out, these descendants? Are they easy to manage? Do they take discipline?

Irving. My God, no! They're stubborn as hell under orders. But wheedle them a little, smooth them the right way, and you can do anything with them.

Stuyvesant. And you say they think well of me, make me out a sort of Manhattan Saint Nicholas?

Irving. That's right.

Stuyvesant. It's worth having. A man doesn't live forever, and he lies a long time in his vault. I'll make a little re-adjustment with the council, and Brom shall not hang. Brom, you shall marry your Tina, and may you raise up a generation of descendants that won't take orders. If that's what they want for Americans that's what they'll get, and the governments to come can worry about it.

Irving. Very handsomely said.

Tina. Brom!

Brom. Tina!

Tina. I've always planned on a large family. Do you mind?

Brom. I shall co-operate in every way possible!

Stuyvesant. And, speaking of Americans, something just occurred to me—

Irving. Yes, sir.

Stuyvesant. Maybe I could qualify. I was never able to take orders!

Irving. That's how you tell an American!

All

[*Sing*]
  It isn't that he's black or white,
  It isn't that he works with tools,
  It's only that it takes away his appetite
  To live by a book of rules.

Yes, it's just that he hates and he damns all the features
Of any mortal man set above his fellow creatures,
And he'll hate the undertaker when at last he dies
If he hears a note of arrogance above him where he lies;
He does his own living, he does his own dying,
Does his loving, does his hating, does his multiplying
Without the supervision of a governmental plan—
And that's an American!

CURTAIN

Epilogue for Stuyvesant

What more remains is but to say
    All characters and all events
Incorporated in our play
    Are fictional in every way,
Nor does one actor here portray
    The person that he represents.

MA.

A